Strategic Studies Institute
and
U.S. Army War College Press

VISUAL PROPAGANDA AND EXTREMISM
IN THE ONLINE ENVIRONMENT

Carol K. Winkler
Cori E. Dauber
Editors

July 2014

*****

CONTENTS

FOREWORD

Most of the papers included in this volume, except for the editor's introduction, come from the conference on Visual Propaganda and Online Radicalization hosted in 2012 by Georgia State University in conjunction with the U.S. Army War College. They all speak to the power of visual images, particularly in the online environment, and the sophistication with which a variety of extremist and terrorist groups have adapted to the online environment, particularly through the use of powerful visual images.

The strategic point made in these essays, and which serves as a unifying theme throughout the collection, is that weaker forces use these materials to great effect, and to even greater effect when we either underestimate the power of visual images or fail to develop effective counters. The unique value offered by these essays is to lay out clearly the ways in which images work for extremist groups, and to begin the process of developing effective strategies for responding. As the editors make clear, there is an extensive literature available establishing that when compared to text (or words heard over an audio track), images are remembered better, over a longer period of time, and with greater emotional power, having commanded more attention initially. This is true for moving and still images.

Today's adversaries have access to technologies that allow them to produce and distribute, with virtually no special training and at very low cost, materials of a quality and sophistication that only a few years ago would have been out of reach of any but professional media labs. Any images available on the web can be repurposed and recontextualized to serve their purposes. In a digital world, the need to respond quickly and effectively is going to be an ever more dominant aspect of any operating environment.

DOUGLAS C. LOVELACE, JR.
Director
Strategic Studies Institute and
   U.S. Army War College Press

CHAPTER 1

RADICAL VISUAL PROPAGANDA IN THE ONLINE ENVIRONMENT: AN INTRODUCTION

Cori E. Dauber
Carol K. Winkler

The presence of terrorist and other extremist groups online has risen sharply over the last 2 decades. In 1998, less than half of the U.S. designated Foreign Terrorist Organizations had websites; by the end of 1999, the number had already jumped to include almost all of them.[1] Between 2003 and 2005, the number of websites serving terrorists and their supporters rose to 4,300.[2] The University of Arizona's Dark Web Project provided a recent snapshot of the substantial traffic operating through online sites associated with extremist groups. In 2011, the Dark Web team reported that they had downloaded the contents of 29 extremist online forums, which resulted in the retrieval of more than 1.5 million conversation threads from more than 350,000 authors who had left 14 million messages.[3]

Many reasons explain why extremist, and particularly terrorist, groups turn to the web. Extremist groups and individuals alike find the online environment to be a relatively cheap, secure, and convenient means of delivery for their communications.[4] The Internet also provides:

> . . . easy access, little to no regulation, censorship or other forms of government control, potentially huge audiences spread throughout the world, anonymity of communication, fast flow of information, interactivity, inexpensive development and maintenance of a Web

presence, a multimedia environment (the ability to combine text, graphics, audio, and video and to allow users to download films, song, book, posters, and so forth), and the ability to shape coverage in the traditional mass media, which increasingly use the Internet as a source for stories.[5]

Further, the online environment can serve as a tool to mobilize a group's resources, as well as a ready channel for depicting a group's violent acts as legitimate, for reaching sympathetic target audiences, and for intimidating opponents.[6]

THE RISE OF EXTREMISTS' VISUAL MEDIA CAMPAIGNS ONLINE

In a revealing letter to former al-Qaeda in Iraq leader Abu Musab al-Zarqawi, al-Qaeda leader Ayman al-Zawahiri provided his reason why a media campaign is part of his group's list of strategic priorities. Al-Zawahiri explained, "More than half of this battle is taking place in the battlefield of the media, . . ."[7] Martin Gurri, Analyst at the Director of National Intelligence Open Source Center, along with two of his colleagues, recall how al-Qaeda implemented its calculated media approach during the Iraq War:

> From the earliest days of the war in Iraq, terrorist and insurgent attacks were regularly staged so that they could be captured on video. In fact, al Qaeda's penchant for spectacular operations can be interpreted as an attempt to persuade the world, using starkly visual argument, of the weakness of western nations and the strength and military superiority of a fearless brand of warriors.[8]

Al-Qaeda and Associated Movements' (AQAM) demonstrated commitment to online media campaigns became particularly evident when U.S. military forces discovered 23 terabytes of video footage in eight media labs in Iraq that members of al-Qaeda in Iraq had yet to upload.[9]

A 2008 random sample of 60 videos retrieved through the Dark Web's spider retrieval approach showed that nine of 10 of their identified jihadist groups used documentary videos to distribute their messages. Among the groups included were Al-Jabha al-Islamiya lil-Muqawama al-'Iraqiya (Islamic Front of the Iraqi Resistance), Al-Jaysh al-Islami fil-'Iraq (Islamic Army in Iraq), Harakat al-Muqawama al-Islamiya fil-'Iraq (Islamic Resistance's Movement in Iraq), Jaysh al-Iraq Al-Islami (Iraq Islamic Army), Jaysh al-Jihad Al-Islami (Islamic Jihad Army), Jaysh al-Mujahidin (Mujahidin's Army), Jaysh al-Ta'ifa al-Mansoura (Victorious Group's Army), Jaysh Ansar al-Sunna (Partisans of the Sunna Army), and Tandhim al-Qa'ida fi Bilad al-Rafidayn (al-Qaeda's Organization in Mesopotamia).[10]

Yariv Tsfati and Gabriel Weimann enumerate an even more globally diversified range of such groups with an online presence, a number of which are secular. Their list includes:

> . . . Hamas, the Lebanese Hizbollah, the Egyptian Al-Gama'a al Islamiyya, the Popular Front for the Liberation of Palestine, the Palestinian Islamic Jihad, the Peruvian Tupak-Amaru and "The Shining Path" (Sendero Luminoso), the Kahane Lives movement, the Basque ETA movement, the Irish Republican Army, "Supreme Truth" (Aum Shinrikyo), the Colombian National Liberation Army, the Liberation Tigers of Tamil Eelam, the Armed Revolutionary Forces of Co-

lombia, the Popular Democratic Liberation Front Party in Turkey, the Kurdish Workers' Party, the Zapatista National Liberation Army, the Japanese Red Army, and the Islamic Movement of Uzbekistan.[11]

In short, terrorist and other extremist groups based around the globe have discovered and begun to capitalize on the online environment to help accomplish their objectives.

Currently, not all extremist groups have the skills necessary to make the most of the Internet's communicative potential. Jialun Qin, Yilu Zhou, and Hsinchun Chen's 2011 comparison of technical proficiency levels reveals the relative abilities of extremist groups based in different regions around the globe:

> [T]he Middle Eastern extremist organizations are the most active exploiters of the Internet. They demonstrated the highest level of technical sophistication and provided the richest multimedia contents in their Web sites. However, due to their covert nature, they did not perform as well as the U.S. domestic extremist organizations in terms of supporting communications using Internet technologies . . . The Latin American groups, on the other hand, lagged behind groups from the other two regions in terms of exploiting the Internet.[12]

While today's Middle Eastern terrorist and other extremist groups provide the richest source of media campaign material for analysis, cheap and easy access to modernized communication technologies virtually assures continued improvements in global extremist groups' future use of visual media campaigns.

The rapid expansion of YouTube provides an additional key factor contributing to the rise of extremists' media campaigns in the online environment. In

April 2005, YouTube uploaded its first video. By July 2006, the site averaged 65,000 uploaded videos a day. By March 2010, YouTube added 24 hours of new video every *minute*.[13] By May 2012, that figure had risen even farther, to 60 hours a minute. Put in perspective, "More video is uploaded to YouTube in 1 month than the 3 major U.S. networks created in 60 years."[14] Paralleling the expansion of the site's content, the size of the YouTube audience both at home and abroad has grown exponentially. The ease of viewing and downloading videos on cell phones, tablets, and other mobile devices rapidly swelled the YouTube audience. During 2011 alone, the site had recorded more than one trillion views, a figure equivalent to 140 views for each person on earth with 70 percent of those coming from outside the United States.[15]

YouTube's community guidelines prohibit videos featuring bomb making, accidents, graphic or gratuitous violence, dead bodies, or similar items intended to shock or disgust. Nevertheless, extremist groups' videos continue to appear on both the YouTube website and other video sharing sites.[16] One recent study of "Web 2.0" applications finds:

> YouTube returned 265 video IDs based on our selected Jihadist extremist terms. Among them, 34% are deemed relevant to cyber extremism. Many of the videos are relevant to explosives, attacks, bombing, hostage taking, and such.[17]

The same study reports how a video's appearance on YouTube aids the distribution goals of extremist groups. Online videos "are mirrored hundreds of times at different websites or forums within a matter of days."[18] The ability of viewers to repost the original or edited versions of content, coupled with the ease of downloading videos to share, renders YouTube's community guidelines and enforcement policy ineffective deterrents for extremist groups. The need to carefully examine the media campaigns of extremist groups, however, reaches beyond the size and reach of their message output.

PROPAGANDA AND EXTREMIST MEDIA CAMPAIGNS ONLINE

Increasingly, a number of extremist and terrorist groups are also demonstrating heightened sophistication in the strategic crafting of their online appeals. Only a few years ago, extremist groups and individuals sympathetic to their causes tended to upload amateur videos that generally lacked much message coherence and clarity. Today, however:

> . . . insurgents adopt similar approaches to state SC [Strategic Communications]. They repeat branded messages that target various tiers of audience. These may address local problems. They may be national, depicting failures of government, highlighting state agencies' direct or proxy attacks on family and livelihood. Moreover they may appeal to wider global constituencies. Mindful of diaspora communities, united by religion, ethnicity or nationality, higher values of faith, community and destiny are called upon. All are swathed in easily identifiable brand philosophy that captures narratives of historical grievance and suffering.[19]

In short, contemporary extremists' online media campaigns represent an ever-improving propaganda effort to engage the "hearts and minds" of their target audiences.

Propaganda is a form of directed persuasion that places the intent of the speaker or propagandist at the center of inquiry. The U.S. Department of Defense (DoD) defines propaganda as:

> Any form of adversary communication, especially of a biased or misleading nature, designed to influence the opinions, emotions, attitudes, or behavior of any group in order to benefit the sponsor, either directly or indirectly.[20]

The distinctive features separating propaganda from persuasion involve intent, form, and function. Related scholarship describes persuasion as an interactive process that seeks mutual recognition, engagement, and consensus between speaker and audience, while describing propaganda as directed or intentional attempts to "disseminate or promote particular ideas."[21] Early studies proposed propaganda as a top-down transaction, but more recent inquiries present propaganda as a two-way transaction in which elite propagandizing interacts with target audiences who play an active role in the production of meaning.[22] For some, propaganda refers to methods that direct, reinforce, and activate public consciousness and participation in a particular belief structure or activity. Its methods combine psychological manipulation with the selective release of information to generate the desired outcome.[23]

Propaganda effects are best understood as audience outcomes that occur over time. The oft-repeated "magic bullet" or "hypodermic needle" theory, whereby scholars, governmental actors or other observers presume specific messages alter the perceptions of passive audience members, generally lacks rigorous research support. In 1955, communication researchers Elihu Katz and Paul Lazarsfeld articulated a more apt, defensible, and lasting view when they described the appropriate parameters for the study of propaganda effects. They stressed a focused consideration on "how, and under what conditions, mass media 'campaigns' (rather than specific, short-run efforts) succeed in influencing opinions and attitudes."[24] While early accounts of propaganda did articulate certain significant effects claims, many researchers today suggest "propaganda confirms rather than converts" and, for that reason, plays a powerful role in short-term, crisis situations like the outbreak of war, but is much less significant over the long term.[25]

Whether propaganda functions to reinforce preexisting views or to change attitudes, beliefs, and behavior over the long term, the need for ongoing studies of extremist online propaganda remains important. Perhaps the most compelling reason is the recurrent presence of terrorist groups' media campaign videos found with individuals arrested for planning or carrying out such acts of violence. Take, for example, the 46 federal cases filed between September 11, 2001, to December 31, 2009, against groups or individuals involved with "domestic radicalization and recruitment to jihadist terrorism" in the United States.[26] Between 2004 and 2009, federal prosecutors tried cases or completed plea bargains with more than 100 individuals in connection with those 46 cases. During those legal proceedings, the U.S. Government referenced videos found in the defendants' possession at the time of their arrests in 53 percent of those individual cases to provide support for the prosecution.[27] Examples outside of the United States further reinforce the linkage between the extremist videos and terrorist acts.[28] While the videos were unlikely to have radicalized those arrested on their own, the recurrent linkage between the groups' media campaign materials and those engaged in terrorist acts remains difficult to ignore.

POWER OF THE IMAGE

So why analyze online visual propaganda? Simply put, understanding the full meaning of posted videos and many other online communications necessitates it. As political media expert Doris Graber notes:

> Purely verbal analyses not only miss the information contained in the pictures and nonverbal sounds, they even fail to interpret the verbal content appropriately because that content is modified by its combination with picture messages.[29]

In short, understanding visual imagery helps avoid drawing incomplete or misleading conclusions about the messages embedded in extremist online media campaigns.

The basis for the visual image, vision itself, is biological and is therefore universal across cultures.[30] The vast majority of human beings process that which they see and the way they experience the world visually, which in turn, is a function of the way the eye and the brain work together. The structure of the eye, and the way it responds to light and to movement, constrains the process of interpreting images to a great extent.[31] Humans process images more quickly than text, making images more emotionally visceral and responses to images frequently more immediate and powerful than responses to text.[32]

Previous research related to broadcast news and political campaigns documents various ways that images influence viewers. To begin, such studies report that visual images function to attract viewer attention. When a video's visual and auditory tracks present conflicting information in experimental conditions, for example, viewers pay more attention to the visual.[33] Viewers focus on visual information because they see images as credible records, allowing them to "witness" news events even though they themselves were not physically present.[34] Images also draw attention because viewers process the complex, visual detail of images simultaneously, rather than engage in the more challenging, sequential approach needed to process verbal information.[35] Finally, visual images attract viewer attention because they stimulate emotional responses, particularly in those that depict violence, mutilated bodies, or war casualties.[36]

Visual images not only attract the attention of viewers, but they also expand the audience base for the messages of media campaigns. Images can attract the attention of younger or illiterate audience members who lack sufficient reading skills for efficient processing of written text.[37] As many terrorist and other extremist groups target audiences from regions with large youth populations and high illiteracy rates in their online propaganda campaigns, understanding visual message strategies becomes an imperative for realizing the full extent of what such groups are communicating.[38]

Beyond increasing both the attention and the potential size of target audiences, the use of visual images in persuasive campaigns also heightens message recall. Experimental studies demonstrate that viewers recall visual information at higher rates than information that either auditory or textual channels deliver.[39] Scholars explain why by noting that viewers appear to bypass logic and accept images at face value. Text, by contrast, "consists of claims, warrants, and evidence, which people are trained to resist."[40] Of course, viewers do not typically see or process visual images in isolation. More typically, they see images presented in combination with captions, audio soundtracks, or other textual material. If visual images reinforce the auditory track of a video, studies show that viewers more clearly remember the information conveyed.[41] If images contradict the auditory channel of a message, however, viewers recall more visual than auditory information.[42]

Not all images contribute to enhanced viewer recall equally. Viewers are more likely to recall information that is redundant across both visual and verbal channels.[43] Specific elements of visual imagery, such as level of emotional content, type of editing, and the pacing of the visual presentation, all contribute to differential viewer recall of messages.[44] For example, some studies find that negative images in broadcast television news contribute to higher recall of both the story associated with the image and the entire newscast in which producers embedded the story.[45] Others, testing a theory of limited capacity, conclude: "compelling negative images retroactively *inhibit* memory for material that precedes them, while they proactively *enhance* memory for material that follows them."[46]

Heightened viewer attention and recall, however, would be of little consequence if visual images did not have some demonstrable influence on the attitudes, beliefs, or behaviors of viewers. Some maintain that viewers simply do not change their views based on visual propaganda. Consider, for example, Yael Warshel's ethnographic study of 5- to 8-year-old Palestinian and Israeli children. The study evaluates the impact of *Sesame Street* programming designed to foster more positive views of the "other" by an inclusion of embedded Israeli and Palestinian characters that were kind and giving. The *Sesame Street* images appeared to reinforce, rather than change, existing views, as Israeli children did not "see" characters with positive valances as Palestinian. Likewise, Palestinian children did not "see" characters with positive valances as Israeli. They simply assumed that the positive characters came from their own groups.[47] Another documented reason some studies conclude that visual images do not change viewer attitudes or behaviors is that they find the images distracting.[48]

Many studies, however, show that negative images do change the attitudes of viewers. One experimental study of college-aged American students watching network television news coverage of combat operations in Iraq revealed:

> . . . television news stories featuring visual footage of combat reduced viewers' pride about US military presence in Iraq, enhanced their involvement levels about the war, and reduced viewers' support for continued US military presence in Iraq.[49]

Studies also document that viewers react to disturbing images by changing their views of the world, by becoming more fearful or anxious, by amplifying their perceptions of risk, and by adopting revised assessments of the consequences of what the image depicts.[50]

To summarize, not all images have persuasive power, which helps explain the seemingly contradictory results of earlier studies. Some images appear, but are forgotten quickly or distract viewers. Others resonate for a time with certain groups, but have differential or no meaning with audience members who harbor competing perspectives. Certain images function as part of influential media campaigns, with their import only knowable within broader audio, textual, and visual message contexts. An important few have a lasting impact as markers for certain collectives, cultures, or nationalities. Given that previous studies of television news report that visual elements of broadcast news reinforce ideology in "ways that differ from written, oral or cinematic modes of embedding,"[51] more nuanced empirical examinations are necessary to fully understand the power of the image-based extremist propaganda online.

Despite the extensive body of research documenting the power of visual images to influence viewers in various ways, previous work on the online presence of extremist and terrorist groups has, for the most part, placed a clear emphasis on understanding the words contained in the groups' messages rather than images.[52] A few exceptions, however, are noteworthy. *The Islamic Imagery Project: Visual Motifs in Jihadi Internet Propaganda* identifies recurrent images used in the propaganda of jihadist groups and offers abbreviated explanations of the likely meaning of those images for target audiences.[53] Arab Salem, Edna Reid, and Hsinchun Chen add a content analysis of 265 videos, categorizing them for location, type, and target of attacks, as well as for presence or absence of special effects, logos, hymns, and leaders' speeches. They also classify the videos as serving operational or nonoperational goals, as well as individual or group goals.[54]

Hanna Rogan's *Al-Qaeda's Online Media Strategies: From Abu Reuter to Irhabi 007* analyzes the online media campaign of al-Qaeda from September to December 2006.[55] She concludes:

Jihadist online media is used for framing and agenda setting, and facilitates the accomplishment of a number of strategic goals of communication, . . . The jihadist online media campaign appears, so far, to be a driving force for the maintenance and development of the movement, as it spreads the messages of global jihadism, invites individuals to participate, educates, and creates and preserves bonds between various factions of the movement.[56]

While Rogan's analysis provides important insights regarding how online media campaigns contribute to the causes of extremist groups, the role of visual argument in her analysis is lost as she does not explicate the independent contribution of the visual, aural, and textual messages within her overall findings.

Finally, Neville Bolt's *The Violent Image: Insurgent Propaganda and the New Revolutionaries* offers one of the most recent examinations of extremist groups' visual propaganda efforts.[57] Bolt analyzes the extremists' use of what he calls "propaganda of the deed" (POTD), a label he places on acts of violence staged to create media events for the purpose of social transformation or revolution. He finds that insurgent groups use images of their terrorist acts as a "way of creating memory through the fragmentation of time and the manipulation of the grievance narrative."[58] Bolt's book stresses the importance of understanding extremist propaganda as strategic communication and the need for extensive future study.

Here, we will add to the nascent literature on the use of visual imagery in the online environment by examining message circulation, strategies, and interpretative frameworks as means for understanding terrorist and other extremist propaganda. Before presenting an outline of the authors' contributions to the volume, we will first describe our definitional parameters for the term "extremism."

DEFINING EXTREMISM

Defining clear boundaries for what constitutes extremism poses a difficult challenge. International actors, U.S. Government officials, scholarly communities, and even the authors who have written chapters for this book do not agree on the meaning of the term. Nor does the DoD, the Department of the Army, or the Department of Homeland Security define extremism in their official publications or doctrinal statements. For the purposes of this volume, extremism will include the activities of terrorists, violent hate groups, and radical groups. Our purpose in identifying these subcategories is to reveal the range of activities discussed here rather than to draw sharp dividing lines between the three, as examples from each group frequently carry the labels of the others in both public and popular discourse.

Terrorists.

Title 22 of the U.S. Code, Section 2656f(d)2 defines terrorism as "premeditated, politically motivated violence perpetrated against noncombatant targets by subnational groups or clandestine agents."[59] Common examples of groups whose activities would be covered by this definition include Aum Shinrikyo, who perpetrated the subway sarin gas attack in Tokyo in 1995; the Irish Republican Army, who conducted the Bloody Friday bombings in Belfast in 1972; and al-Qaeda, who executed the suicide plane assaults on the World Trade Center, the Pentagon, and Shanksville, Pennsylvania, in 2001. While the specific groups who qualify for the terrorist label depend on ever-evolving interpretations,[60] U.S. Government-designated foreign terrorist organizations do fall within this volume's conception of extremist groups.

Violent Hate Groups.

Violent hate groups, the second set of extremists included here, encompass ideologically motivated individuals that act in violent ways. The differences between violent hate groups and terrorists (as defined above) are that such groups base themselves within U.S. boundaries, and their goals are to malign entire classes of people responsible for perceived social ills, rather than society as a whole. Examples of groups convicted as violent hate groups include the White Aryan Resistance, the United Klan of America, the White Patriot Party, and Aryan Nation.

Radicalized Groups.

Finally, this book discusses radicalized groups, where the majority of their members have yet to act on their views by engaging in acts of violence. While the original meaning of a radical was to get to the root of a social problem, today radicalization has emerged as "the process of developing extremist ideologies and beliefs."[61] The actual motivation to participate in these groups is not necessarily ideological or religious, but oftentimes instead, economical, political, or social.[62] Examples of radicalized groups that could also qualify as extremist include anti-abortion groups, anti-globalization groups, environmental groups, and a myriad of religious sects both at home and abroad.

Propaganda and Extremism.

Each of the authors in this volume discusses visual propaganda and online extremism within the broad parameters of terrorist groups, violent hate groups, or radical groups described here. While a typical volume would adhere to a unified definition of key terms, this book, instead, provides our authors the opportunity to define extremism in line with their own views and within their own study's parameters. Each chapter does focus on nonstate actors, but the location of operational bases for the extremist groups varies from the United States to the Middle East, Africa, and the former Soviet Union. Given the comparative sophistication of the use of visual propaganda by groups based in the Middle East noted above, the bulk of the chapters will examine products, by group, that Middle East groups have produced. We assume the study on any one region or any one group provides insights that will inform future contexts around the globe, as dispersed groups will likely borrow strategies from the more sophisticated groups.

Plan for the Book.

Building on ideas presented at Georgia State University's 2012 *Visual Propaganda and Online Radicalization Conference* held in conjunction with the U.S. Army War College's Academic Engagement Program, this book provides theoretical and practical approaches for studying how extremist groups use visual media campaigns in their online propaganda efforts. It discloses many online visual strategies that such groups use to reach their target audiences, provides cautionary reminders of the importance of context for evaluating image campaigns, and offers suggestions for how to understand and respond to the powers of images in productive ways.

The first section of the book includes two studies that explore how image recirculation can aid understandings of extremist propaganda and options for appropriate response. Each author examines a specific group of recycled historical images to help explain what factors give certain images lasting resonance with targeted audiences. By identifying visual strategies that both succeeded and failed to achieve lasting resilience, these studies provide insights for which online messages are worthy of response and what parameters should help shape those approaches.

In Chapter 1, Anne Stenerson of the Norwegian Defense Research Institute illustrates the importance of examining historical court documents and related media coverage of those found guilty of terrorism-related offenses for understanding the visual propaganda of jihadist groups. She describes recurrent strategies in the videos jihadists viewed, shared, or accumulated in cases adjudicated in Europe, Canada, and the United States since 2001. Based on her preliminary analysis of 18 court cases, she identifies particular time periods of video release and certain image patterns that reveal the viewing preferences of the most radicalized members of these groups.

In Chapter 2, Carol K. Winkler of Georgia State University examines historical images of national apology to theorize the strategic considerations in play when responding to offending images circulating in the online environment. She begins by focusing attention on three visual image strategies particularly deserving of response, tracing how these approaches have a documented, lasting resonance for viewers. She then uses circulating images in the present day associated with historical national apologies from around the globe to illustrate a needed shift in response strategy. She advocates for a visual reconciliation approach instead of face-saving apologies to answer enduring offending images online.

The second section of the book focuses on analyzing the visual messaging strategies contemporary extremists employ to convey their messages. The studies highlight how visual images strategically reinforce identifiable themes, narratives, or brands of groups operating both in and outside of the United States. The authors stress that the recurrent implementation of these strategies functions as a key means used to form identity for their respective groups.

In Chapter 3, Michael Waltman of the University of North Carolina at Chapel Hill analyzes the online communication approach of white violent hate groups operating in the United States. He begins by providing an overview of the core beliefs of the three dominant groups he investigates in his study: followers of the Christian Identity Church, pre-Christian Pagans, and the Militia movement. Afterwards, he reports how such groups use visual imagery to define the value of their in-group members, to denigrate out-groups, and to justify violence when necessary to vanquish threats to their culture.

In Chapter 4, Scott Ruston and Jeffry Halverson, both of Arizona State University's Center for Strategic Communication, describe how visual images contribute to the narratives of online propaganda efforts of jihadist groups. Comparing videos by media production and distribution wings of official terrorist organizations (e.g., *As-Sahab* and *Al-Malahim*) with those from fan-based "jihobbyists," they evaluate the form, content, and narrative landscape used to sway their target audiences. They conclude by recommending that the Department of State's Digital Outreach Team employ a strategy of alternative, rather than competing, narratives in the development of its information campaign.

In Chapter 5, Cori E. Dauber of the University of North Carolina at Chapel Hill scrutinizes the visual branding strategies of AQAM. She describes how AQAM uses logos to establish brand loyalty by applying empirical findings of marketing research. She then identifies characteristic design and animated short elements that recur in AQAM logos and explains the persuasive potential of those features. Recognizing that her use of marketing studies renders her findings preliminary, she concludes by calling for empirical, audience-based studies of AQAM's visual branding strategies.

The final section of the book focuses on revised approaches for analyzing audience effects of online visual images. The chapters describe the limitations of conventional perspectives for predicting viewer response and suggest that, rather than abandoning the earlier approaches, adding complementary frameworks would improve analysis of extremist propaganda.

In Chapter 6, Shawn Powers from Georgia State University, and Matt Armstrong, member of the Broadcasting Board of Governors, examine how a focus on the broader context of transnational public spheres should transform understandings of radical messaging strategies. They recommend that policymakers should turn away from propaganda or dialogic theories of communication effectiveness. Instead, they should consider that online radicalization functions within a "marketplace of loyalties," whereby participants play roles as buyers and sellers that have different needs and agencies. Their chapter concludes with implications of such a perspective for defining what messages qualify as radical, for negotiating what constitutes an authority in the online environment, and for how nation-states should respond to transnational appeals for their citizens.

In Chapter 7, Saeid Balkesim of Georgia State University provides an alternative computer programming approach for the efficient and productive retrieval of online extremist images and the audiences who receive them. He begins by critiquing current syntactical methods of image retrieval as unable to capture extremists' use of manipulated or partial images. Instead, he offers and describes a semantic retrieval approach that retains the advantages of the current syntactical approach, while supporting multiple data formats, strengthening partial object retrieval, and offering an evolving, dynamic retrieval system that responds to the needs of responders.

In Chapter 8, Natalia Mielczarek of the University of Iowa and David Perlmutter of Texas Tech University, examine historical images of photojournalists covering wars in an effort to better understand the likely impact images in extremist and terrorist propaganda have on viewers. Drawing from studies from the fields of psychology and mass communication, they emphasize that while certain iconic images do have power(s) in particular circumstances, contextual factors related to the audience and perceptions about the audience's reactions are crucial elements in assessing pictures' impact. They conclude with a series of recommendations for those seeking to counter extremists' visual appeals.

As even this preview of chapters illustrates, this volume covers a myriad of topics related to visual propaganda and online extremism. As a result, the chapters may, at first glance, appear to have more or less relevance to any given reader. We suggest, however, that the parallel uses of visual propaganda across the various case studies merits a closer look. Findings tied to particular contexts may function fruitfully as testable hypotheses for new situations. This collection of essays should be a beginning, rather than an end to the conversation about the use of visual imagery in extremist propaganda in the online environment. Extremist groups are highly unlikely to have less of a presence online in the years to come or to use visual images less aggressively in their propaganda campaigns.

ENDNOTES - CHAPTER 1

1. Gabriel Weimann, *Terror on the Internet: The New Arena, The New Challenges,* Washington, DC: United States Institute of Peace Press, 2006.

2. *Ibid.*

3. Hsinchun Chen, Dorothy Denning, Nancy Roberts N, Cathy A. Larson, Ximing, Yu, Chun-Heng Huang, *Proceedings on the 2011 Institute of Electrical and Electronics Engineers (IEEE) International Conference on Intelligence and Security Informatics,* Inter-Service Intelligence (ISI), Beijing, China, July 2011, pp. 7-14.

4. Tianjun Fu, Chun-Neng Huang, and Hsinchun Chen, "Identification of Extremist Videos in Online Video Sharing Sites," *Proceedings on the 2009 IEEE International Conference on Intelligence and Security Informatics,* ISI, 2009, pp. 179-181.

5. Weimann, p. 31.

6. Hsinchun Chen, Sven Thomas, Tianjun Fu, "Cyber Extremism in Web 2.0: An Exploratory Study of International Jihadist Groups," *Proceedings on the 2008 IEEE International Conference on Intelligence and Security Informatics,* ISI, 2008, pp. 98-103.

7. Ayman al-Zawahiri quoted in "Internet Jihad: A World Wide Web of Terror," *The Economist,* Vol. 384, July 14, 2007, p. 29.

8. Martin Gurri, Craig Denny, and Aaron Harms, "Our Visual Persuasion Gap," *Parameters,* Vol. 40, No. 1, Spring 2010, p. 103.

9. Cori E. Dauber, *YouTube War: Fighting in a World of Cameras in Every Cell Phone and Photoshop on Every Computer,* Carlisle, PA: Strategic Studies Institute, U.S. Army War College, November 2009.

10. Arab Salem, Edna Reid, and Hsinchun Chen, "Multimedia Content Coding and Analysis: Unraveling the Content of Jihadi Extremist Groups' Videos," *Studies in Conflict and Terrorism,* Vol. 31, 2008, p. 614.

11. Yariv Tsfati and Gabriel Weimann, "www.terorrism.com: Terror on the Internet," *Studies in Conflict and Terrorism,* Vol. 23, 2002, pp. 317-332.

12. Jialun Qin, Yilu Zhou, and Hsinchun Chen, "A Multi-Region Empirical Study of the Internet Presence of Global Extremist Organizations," *Information Systems Frontiers,* Vol. 13, No. 1, 2011, p. 87.

13. "Timeline," available from *www.youtube.com/t/press_timeline.*

14. YouTube, "Statistics," available from *www.youtube.com/t/press_statistics.*

15. *Ibid.*

16. YouTube Community Guidelines, available from *www.youtube.com/t/community_guidelines.* Terrorist and other extremist groups can take advantage of YouTube and similar sites by hiding their material in plain sight. Literally tens of thousands of vid-

eos supportive of the AQAM message are available on YouTube, spanning the spectrum from simple sermons preaching a message supportive of violence to actual beheadings. Most of these videos violate YouTube's stated policies, but for them to be pulled from the site, someone has to view and object to them, understand the complaint policy, and go to the effort of filing a complaint. The likelihood of that is extremely low and, once pulled, reposts of the same content can re-circulate under another name.

17. Chen, Thomas, and Fu, 2008, p. 102.

18. *Ibid.*, p. 16.

19. Neville Bolt, *Violent Image: Insurgent Propaganda and the New Revolutionaries,* New York: Columbia University Press, 2012, p. 50.

20. Joint Chiefs of Staff, "Propaganda," *Joint Publication (JP) 3-13.2: Psychological Operations,* Washington, DC: Department of Defense, p. GL-7, available from *www.fas.org/irp/doddir/dod/jp 3-13-2.pdf.*

21. Garth S. Jowett and Victoria O'Donnell, *Propaganda and Persuasion,* Thousand Oaks, CA: Sage Publications, Fifth Ed., 2011, pp. 1-2.

22. *Ibid.*, pp. 11-12.

23. David R. Wilcox, *Propaganda, The Press, and Conflict: The Gulf War and Kosovo,* New York: Routledge, 2005, p. 13.

24. Elihu Katz and Paul F. Lazarsfeld, *Personal Influence,* Glencoe, IL: Free Press, 1955, p. 19. For a more extensive historical review of the growth and perspectives of propaganda studies and implementation, see J. Michael Sproule, "Progressive Propaganda Critics and the Magic Bullet Myth," *Critical Studies in Mass Communication,* Vol. 6, No. 3, September 1989, pp. 225-246; J. Michael Sproule, "Propaganda Studies in American Social Science: The Rise and Fall of the Critical Paradigm," *Quarterly Journal of Speech,* Vol. 73, No. 2, February 1987, pp. 60-79; and Colonel Calvin C. DeWitt, "Strategic Communication, Psychological Operations and Propaganda: Is a Unified Message Possible," *Information as Power, 2009.*

25. David Welch, "Introduction: Propaganda in Histori-cal Perspective," Nicholas J. Cull, David Culbert, and David Welch, eds., *Propaganda and Mass Persuasion: A Historical Ency-clopedia, 1500 to the Present,* Santa Barbara, CA: ABC-CLIO, 2003, pp. xviii, xx.

26. As chronicled by Brian Michael Jenkins, "Would-Be War-riors: Incidents of Jihadist Terrorist Radicalization in the United States since September 11, 2001," Santa Monica, CA: 2010, avail-able from, *www.rand.org/pubs/occasional_papers/OP292.html.*

27. The editors would like to thank Stephen Heidt, Presiden-tial Fellow of Transcultural Conflict and Violence, Georgia State University, for analyzing all the related court documents.

28. Just two of the most well-known examples from Europe are that of Roshonara Choudhry, arrested for attempting to stab a Member of Parliament to death after watching videos on You-Tube (see Vikram Dodd, "Roshonara Choudhry: Police Interview Extracts," *The Guardian*, November 3, 2010, available from *www. guardian.co.uk/uk/2010/nov/03/roshonara-choudhry-police-interview*), and Arid Uka, arrested after shooting American airmen at the Frankfurt airport, also after having seen videos on YouTube (see "Kosovan Admits Shooting US Airmen At Frankfurt Airport," *BBC News Europe*, August 31, 2011, available from *www.bbc.co.uk/ news/world-europe-14727975*). After the Choudhry episode, a rep-resentative of the British government went to Washington to ap-peal directly to the U.S. Government to pressure Google, which owns YouTube, to demand stricter controls and to pull more videos from the site. The plot to attack the United States with bombs hidden in cargo planes strengthened the appeal (see John F. Burns and Miguel Helft, "YouTube Withdraws Clerics Videos," *New York Times*, November 3, 2010, available from *www.nytimes. com/2010/11/04/world/04britain.html?_r=0*). Awlaki's banishment from the site lasted no more than a few weeks at best, and now thousands of videos featuring him are back on the site.

29. Doris A. Graber, "Content and Meaning, What's It All About?" *American Behavioral Scientist,* Vol. 33, No. 2, 1980, p. 145.

30. Donald D. Hoffman, *Visual Intelligence: How We Create What We See*, New York: W. W. Norton and Company, 1998.

31. Richard L. Gregory, *Eye and Brain: The Psychology of Seeing*. Princeton, NJ: Princeton University Press, 1966.

32. Michael Pfau, Michael Haigh, Andreelynn Fifrick, Douglas Holl, Allison Tedesco, Jay Cope, David Nunnally, Amy Schiess, Donald Preston, Paul Roszkowski, and Marlon Martin, "The Effects of Print News Photographs on the Casualties of War," *Journalism and Mass Communication Quarterly*, Vol. 83, No. 1, Spring 2006, pp. 150-168.

33. Dan G. Drew and Thomas Grimes, "Audio-visual Redundancy and TV News Recall," *Communication Research*, Vol. 14, No. 4, August 1987, pp. 452-461.

34. Marshall McLuhan and Quentin Fiore, *The Medium is the Message: An Inventory of Effects*, New York: Bantam Books, 1967, p. 117.

35. Doris A. Graber, "Seeing is Remembering: How Visuals Contribute to Learning From Television News," *Journal of Communication*, Vol. 40, No. 3, Summer 1990, pp. 134-155; Pfau *et al.*, "The Effects of Print News Photographs on the Casualties of War," pp. 150-168.

36. *Ibid.*, p. 161; Ann Marie Barry, *Visual Intelligence: Perception, Image, and Manipulation in Visual Communication*, Albany, NY: State University of New York Press, 1997; Robin L. Naboi, "'Feeling,' Resistance: Exploring the Role of Emotionally Evocative Visuals in Inducing Inoculation," *Media Psychology*, Vol. 5, No. 2, May 2003, pp. 199-223; Annie Lang and John Newhagen, "Negative Video as Structure: Emotion, Attention, Capacity, and Memory, *Journal of Broadcasting and Electronic Media*, Vol. 40, No. 4, Fall 1996, pp. 460-477.

37. Doris A. Graber, "Say It With Pictures," *Annals of the American Academy of Political and Social Sciences*, Vol. 546, July 1996, p. 86.

38. For illiteracy rates in specific countries, see "Adult Illiteracy Rates," New York: United Nations. For youth projections in Muslim areas worldwide, see the Pew Forum on Religion and Public Life, "The Future of the Global Muslim Population: Projections from 2010-2030," available from *www.pewforum.org/future-of-the-global-muslim-population-regional-middle-east.aspx*.

39. Robert Hariman and John Lucaites, "Public Identity and Collective Memory in U.S. Iconic Photography: The Image of 'Accidental Napalm,'" *Critical Studies in Media Communication,* Vol. 20, No. 1, March 2003, pp. 35-66; David Perlmutter, *Photojournalism and Foreign Policy: Icons of Outrage in International Crisis,* Westport, CT: Praeger, 1998.

40. Pfau *et al.,* "Print News Photographs," p. 161.

41. Drew and Grimes, 1987; Julia R. Fox, "A Signal Detection Analysis of Audio/Video Redundancy Effects in Television News Video," *Communication Research,* Vol. 31, No. 5, October 2004, pp. 524-536; Annie Lang, "Defining Audio/Video Redundancy From a Limited-Capacity Information Processing Perspective, *Communication Research,* Vol. 22, No. 1, February 1995, pp. 86-115.

42. Drew and Grimes, 1987.

43. Barrie Gunter, "Remembering News Effects of Picture Content," *The Journal of General Psychology,* Vol. 102, 1980, pp. 127-133; Annie Lang, "Defining Audio/Video Redundancy from a Limited-Capacity Information Processing Perspective," *Communication Research,* Vol. 1, No. 1, 1995, pp. 86-115.

44. Michael D. Basil, "Multiple Resource Theory 1: Application to Television Viewing," *Communication Research,* Vol. 21, No. 2, April 1994, pp. 177-207; Lang, 1985; Annie Lang, Deborah Potter, and Maria Elizabeth Grabe, "Making News Memorable: Applying Theory to the Production of Local Television News," *Journal of Broadcasting & Electronic Media,* Vol. 47, No. 1, March, 2003, pp. 113-121.

45. See, for example, Graber, "Seeing is Remembering," 1990; John P. Robinson and Mark R. Levy, *The Main Source: Learning from Television News*, Beverly Hills, CA: Sage, 1986.

46. John E. Newhagen and Byron Reeves, "The Evening's Bad News: Effects of Compelling Negative Television News Images on Memory," *Journal of Communication*, Vol. 42, No. 2, Spring 1992, p. 25.

47. Yael Warshal, "How Do You Convince Children that the 'Army,' 'Terrorists,' and the 'Police' Can Live Together Peacefully? A Peace Communication Assessment Model," Dissertation Abstracts, UMI Number 3386931, Ann Arbor, MI: University Microfilms International, 2009.

48. Mickie Edwardson, Donald Grooms, and Suzanne Proudlove, "Visualization and TV News Information Gain," *Journal of Broadcasting & Electronic Media*, Vol. 25, 1976, pp. 15-24; Norbert Mundorf, Dan Drew, Dolf Zillman, and James Weaver, "Effects of Disturbing News on Recall of Subsequently Presented News," *Communication Research*, Vol. 17, No. 5, October 1990, pp. 601-615.

49. Michael Pfau, Michel M. Haigh, Theresa Shannon, Toni Tones, Deborah Mercurio, Raina Williams, Blanca Binstock, Carlos Diaz, Constance Dillard, Margaret Browne, Clarence Elder, Sherri Reed, Adam Eggers, and Juan Melendez, 'The Influence of Television News Depictions of the Images of War on Viewers," *Journal of Broadcasting and Electronic Media*, Vol. 52, No. 2, p. 318.

50. George Gerbner, Larry Gross, Michael Morgan, and Nancy Signorielli, "The Mainstreaming of American Violence Profile No. 11," *Journal of Communication*, Vol. 30, Summer 1980, pp. 10-29; John E. Newhagen and Marion Lewenstein, "Cultivation and Exposure to Television Following the 1989 Loma Prieta Earthquake," *Mass Communication Review*, Vol. 19, No. 1, 1992, pp. 49-56; Montague Kern, Marion Just, and Pippa Norris, "The Lessons of Framing Terrorism," Pippa Norris, Montague Kern, and Marion Just, eds., *Framing Terrorism: The News Media, the Government, and the Public*, New York: Routledge & Kegan Paul, pp. 281-302; Leonie Huddy, Stanley Feldman, Gallya Lahav, and Charles Taber, "Fear and Terrorism: Psychological Reactions to 9/11," Pippa Norris, Montague Kern, and Marion Just, eds., *Framing Terrorism: The News Media, the Government, and the Public*, New York: Routledge & Kegan Paul, pp. 255-278; Joanne Cantor, "Fright Responses to Mass Media," Bryant Jennings and Dolf Zillman, eds.,

Responding to the Screen, Hillsdale, NJ: Lawrence Erlbaum Associates, 1991, pp. 169-198.

51. Nitzan Ben-Shaul, *A Violent World: TV News Images of Middle Eastern Terror and War,"* Oxford, UK: Rowman and Littlefield, 2006, p. 53.

52. For a few examples, see Jenny Craven and Shelagh, *Extremism and the Internet,* Manchester, UK: Center for Research in Library and Information Management, 1999; Antonio Roversi, *Hate on the Net: Extremist Sites, Neo-Fascism On-line, Electronic Jihad,* Burlington, VT: Ashgate, 2008; Jeffry R. Halverson, *Master Narratives of Islamist Extremism,* New York: Palgrave Macmillan, 2011; Philip Seib, *Global Terrorism and New Media: The Post-Al Qaeda Generation,* New York: Routledge, 2011; Marc Sageman, *Leaderless Jihad: Terror Networks in the Twenty-First Century,* Philadelphia, PA: The University of Pennsylvania Press, 2008; Weimann, 2006; Miriyam Aouragh, *Palestine Online: Transnationalism, the Internet and Construction of Identity,* London, UK: I. B. Taurus, 2001.

53. United States Military Academy, *The Islamic Imagery Project: Visual Motifs in Jihadi Internet Propaganda,* West Point, NY: Combating Terrorism Center, March 2006.

54. Salem, Reid, and Chen, 2008, pp. 605-626.

55. Hanna Rogan, *Al-Qaeda's Online Media Strategies: From Abu Reuter to Irhabi 007,* Kjeller, Norway: Norwegian Defence Research Establishment, 2007, available from *www.ffi.no/no/Rapporter/07-02729.pdf.*

56. *Ibid.,* p. 117.

57. Bolt. Another book unavailable at the writing of this volume that focuses on visual imagery is Lina Khatib, *Image Politics in the Middle East: The Role of the Visual in Political Struggle,* London, UK: I. B. Taurus, 2012.

58. Bolt, p. 257.

59. U.S. Code, Title 22, Section 2565f(d2), U.S., available from *www.state.gov/ documents/organization/65464.pdf.*

60. For a more extensive discussion of terrorism as a cultural marker, see Carol K. Winkler, *In the Name of Terrorism: Presidents on Political Violence in the Post-World War II Era,* Albany, NY: State University of New York Press, 2006.

61. Randy Borum, "Radicalization into Violent Extremism I: A *Review* of Social Science Theories," *Journal of Strategic Security,* Vol. 4, No. 4, 2001, pp. 7-36.

62. Faiza Patel, *Rethinking Radicalization,* New York: New York University of Law: Brennan Center for Justice, 2011.

SECTION I:

PERSPECTIVES ON THE RE-CIRCULATION
OF ONLINE VISUAL IMAGES

CHAPTER 2

GATHERING DATA THROUGH COURT CASES: IMPLICATIONS FOR UNDERSTANDING VISUAL MESSAGING

Anne Stenersen

The jihadi video is one of al-Qaeda's most effective propaganda tools.[1] Al-Qaeda and their associates produce jihadi videos in various parts of the world, and then disseminate them on the Internet. The videos themselves divide into distinct genres, ranging from those dominated by operational footage to those featuring instructions on how to manufacture bombs. While the last category is instrumental in its purpose, a majority of jihadi videos function as emotionally grounded tools of persuasion that attempt to shape the beliefs of potential recruits.

Despite the numerous studies written about al-Qaeda's audiovisual propaganda, most are descriptive in nature, focusing on content, messaging strategies, and target audiences. Few, however, empirically study the way radicals actually use jihadi videos in practice.[2] While the Internet gives access to an abundance of video material, tracking the most viewed videos, who views them, and what effect they have on their audiences is very difficult. Readily available, partial data includes the number of hits a certain video has on a certain webpage and the comments and discussions attached to the video. However, numerous problems with this method result in multiple errors in the final analysis. Most crucially, such approaches do not reveal whether the individuals who accessed these videos were, or will ever become, active jihadists. Moreover, such approaches do not take into account such individuals' exposure to other types of radicalizing factors. Therefore, data gathered exclusively from the Internet is not sufficient to study the effects of al-Qaeda's visual messaging on radicalization.

To overcome this challenge, this chapter uses court documents as its primary source of data. The approach enables the creation of a database of jihadi videos convicted jihadists have in their possession prior to their arrest. Such an approach gives invaluable information about the viewers of these videos—their identity, age, and roles in established terror plots. Occasionally, the court documents provide information about how the jihadist obtained the video, the setting for viewing, and the audience's reactions.

The chapter aims to answer two questions. In the aftermath of 2001, what types of videos do captured jihadists watch? And, is it possible to identify changes in the jihadists' viewer preferences over time? Subsequently, these micro-level data will serve as the foundation of possible hypotheses for why some videos tend to become more popular with active jihadists, while others do not.

Worth noting is the fact that this is not a study of radicalization in general. Jihadi videos may be only one of a number of radicalizing factors in an individual's life. This chapter does not attempt to measure the importance of videos relative to other radicalizing factors. The aim, instead, is to identify how jihadi videos—and their dominant visual images—function within radical environments. For example, are active jihadists drawn to images of "divine rewards," or do they instead gravitate toward images of a "cool" counterculture? Such understanding is essential knowledge for the development of effective countermessaging approaches. For example, if radical environments draw in recruits due to their religious convictions, a counter-message presenting theological arguments for why al-Qaeda's agenda contradicts Islam's teachings might be the most effective. However, if a majority of the recruits are simply seeking adventure, rather than divine rewards, then those involved in counter-messaging must adjust accordingly.

DATA COLLECTION AND CODING

This chapter uses West European, Canadian and U.S. court documents, as well as mainstream media sources quoting information from these court cases, to provide the source material regarding jihadists' video preferences. Data collection for this research project is ongoing, as more sources become available. As of this writing, 18 court cases are available. The chapter breaks down the contents of those cases into "video events," each involving at least one jihadi video that at least one arrested individual obtained, viewed, or shared. Prior to data analysis, the chapter's method excluded all cases of video events in the possession of individuals who authorities arrested but subsequently acquitted.

The quality of the data varies from case to case, depending on the type of documents available, their level of detail, and how much information the arrested individuals themselves volunteered. One challenge in the cataloging of the samples is to identify the videos, their titles, their producers, and their production years. Court documents occasionally provide the information, but usually only partial descriptions are available, such as "videos about the Chechen Mujahideen." To address this challenge, the chapter codes videos according to their title, description, geographic origin, and production year. In cases where court documents do not identify titles, videos still became part of the sample by referring to other available information, such as geographic origin.

Initially, this chapter's classification schema planned to examine the coding category "video genre."[3] However, such a "genre" classification is misleading for this particular study. Important recurrent visual images, such as "the face of a martyr" or "the suffering Muslim" occur across a number of different genres. Even when court documents mention a "martyr video," prediction is impossible as to what exact images producers embedded into the video (i.e., some "martyr videos" contain images of suffering Muslims, while others do not).

While the category "genre" emerged as a nonproductive classification schema, the category "conflict theater" is easier to define. Court documents often give specific, unambiguous information about the conflict theater of the video, even if they do not specify the title. When the purpose of the video appears not to promote a conflict in a specific geographical area, but rather to promote al-Qaeda's "global jihad," the coding scheme utilizes the term "global."

Finally, the database includes information about the person who obtained the video, such as the viewer's age, the date the viewer watched the video, the circumstances of viewing the video, and the viewer's expressed reactions to the video (such as anger, desire for revenge, or admiration). While the analysis still does not provide enough data to draw firm conclusions, it can test the research design and serve as a primer for further studies.

PRELIMINARY ANALYSIS

In the 18 cases discovered in the court cases or their associated media coverage, the related documents revealed 161 video events, with eight removed because authorities later acquitted the person(s) involved in the event of all charges.[4] Of the remaining 153 video events used, the analysis coded 113 by identified conflict theater and 88 others by identified video title. It also coded other data, such as the viewer's age and reaction to the video. However, at this point, the data related to these other data codes were too scant to serve as a sufficient basis for analysis. For example, only 12 of the 153 "video events" contained information about the viewer's emotional reactions to the video. However, two of the coding categories, conflict theaters and video title, provided a foundation useful for future studies.

Figure 2-1 illustrates that authorities most frequently find jihadi videos from Iraq in active jihadist cells. At one level, such a finding is not very surprising. Videos from Iraq are some of the most abundant on the Internet, and the Iraqi conflict has been one of the hottest discussion topics on jihadi forums.[5] In 11 of the 18 court cases, videos from Iraq appeared in court documents or related media coverage. The Amawi case, in particular, contains an unusually large number of Iraqi videos: 43 video events emerged in relation to that case, of which 22 related to videos about Iraq.

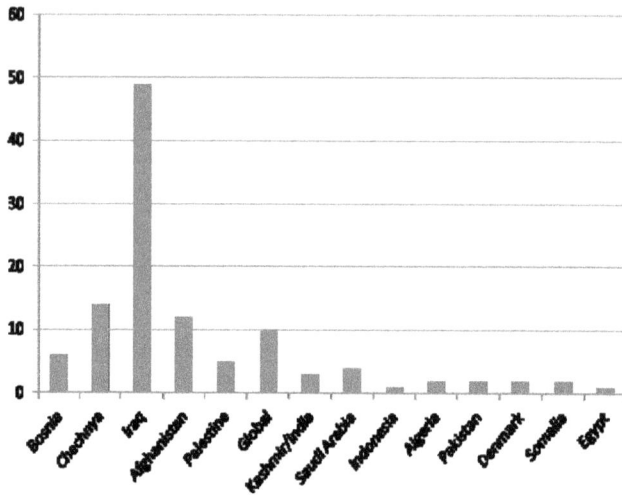

Figure 2-1. Video Events and Conflict Theaters, 1999-2011.

Another purpose of the data analysis was to mea-sure how the jihadis' interest in various conflict the-aters changed over time. Figure 2-2 records only con-flict theaters occurring in five or more video events, with the results sorted by year:

	Bosnia	Chechnya	Iraq	Afghanistan	Palestine	Global
1999	1	1				
2000						
2001	2	4				
2002					1	1
2003	1	1	1	2	2	2
2004	1	3	10	1	1	1
2005	1	2	24	1		2
2006			8	2		3
2007		1	3	1		
2008						
2009				1		
2010			3	1		1
2011		2		3		2

Figure 2-2. Distribution of Geographical Conflict Zones Over Time.

Interest in videos from the Iraq conflict zone peaked in 2004-05. Again, this is not surprising because the Iraq war dominated jihadi discussion forums during the same period. Jihadi videos produced at this time also received attention in the mainstream media — especially the so-called "decapitation videos" al-Qaeda in Iraq (AQI) produced in the latter half of 2004. These videos resembled the video showing the execution of the American journalist Daniel Pearl in Pakistan in 2002. However, 2004 was the first time such videos re-circulated on a large scale and in the context of an ongoing conflict involving U.S. military forces. While some might view the beheading of Daniel Pearl as a one-time event, re-circulated clips of the beheading videos from Iraq emerged as part of a deliberate campaign to deter U.S. military forces from entering the country and to dissuade the American public from supporting the war.[6]

After 2006, the number of "video events" from Iraq declined in the sampled court documents, in spite of the fact that Iraqi jihadists continued to produce a large number of videos. This finding may have been due to the fact that battlefield videos from Iraq were not novel anymore, and therefore they attracted less attention among radicals. AQI had stopped producing "beheading videos" at this point — probably because of a change in media strategy of the al-Qaeda leadership in Pakistan.[7] Moreover, the killing of the charismatic AQI leader Abu Musab al-Zarqawi in 2006, coupled by his anonymous replacement, removed one of the organization's key architects of al-Qaeda's ramped up online media strategy. All of these factors arguably contributed to the decline in "video events" connected to Iraq after 2006.

Notably, the analysis also revealed some counter-intuitive results. First, since 2007, the conflict theaters of Afghanistan, Algeria, and Somalia did not gain much attention. Al-Qaeda associates, such as the Taliban in Afghanistan, Al-Qaeda in the Islamic Maghreb (AQIM) in Algeria, and al-Shabaab in Somalia, have actively produced videos and have maintained a highly visible presence on radical forums online since 2006. On Jihad Archive, an al-Qaeda sympathizer-run digital library of jihadi videos, AQIM's productions occupied the five first places on the "Top 20" list of most viewed videos on the forum in November 2009. Each video had between 3,000 and 5,000 hits.[8] Yet, this heavy traffic did not result in video events in the chapter's court cases.

Second, identifiable active jihadists were still viewing videos from the conflict zone of Chechnya after 2001. The Chechnya videos in the sample do not appear to be new; instead, the videos mostly have their origins in footage shot and edited during the Second Chechen War in 1999-2000. Most of the footage features Samir Saleh Abdullah Al-Suwailem, better known as Emir Khattab, a Saudi Arabian commander Russian forces killed in 2002. Interestingly, despite the fact that Chechen rebels today have an active and professional propaganda campaign in the name of their "Caucasus Emirate" that Chechen rebel leader Dokka Umarov established in 2007, arrested radicals in the Western court cases examined here preferred the previous videos and those praising Commander Khattab. Notably, Khattab was one of the very first jihadi commanders who filmed his own attacks and distributed the tapes to Muslim audiences in the West — before the age of digital cameras and the Internet — and this may have contributed to his fame. Further confirmation of this conclusion emerges when we look at the tallies of the videos in this chapter. (See Figure 2-3.)

Video Title	Producer, Year	Video Event Year
Hell of the Russians 2000	Khattab, 2000	2001, 2001, 2005, 2007
The Destruction of the Destroyer USS *Cole*	As-Sahab, 2001	2003, 2004, 2006
The Martyrs of the Confrontations	AQ/Saudi Arabia, 2004	2004, 2005
The Beheading of an Egyptian Spy	Zarqawi/Iraq, 2004	2005, 2005
The Winds of Victory	Zarqawi/Iraq, 2005	2005, 2006
How to make a Suicide Vest	Hezbollah, 2004	2005, 2006
The Raid of the Muezzin	As-Sahab, 2008	2009, 2009

Figure 2-3. Most Frequently Mentioned Videos in Court Cases.

Of the 88 video events that included identifiable titles, 76 are unique videos. In other words, the radicals identified in these court cases watched a broad spectrum of videos. The only videos mentioned in more than two events are *Hell of the Russians 2000*, and As-Sahab's first major video production, *The Destruction of the Destroyer* USS *Cole* (hereafter referred to as the USS *Cole* video).[9] The fact that arrested radicals in 2006-07 watched and discussed these two videos (produced in 2000 and 2001), instead of others deserves further attention. The rest of the chapter examines this phenomenon in more detail.

Emir Khattab and *The Hell of the Russians 2000*.

The case of Saudi Arabian commander in Chechnya Emir Khattab illustrates how jihadi leaders may survive as iconic figures long after their deaths. Jihadi web forums are full of visual tributes to Khattab in the form of pictures, posters, and videos. Part of the reason simply could be that Khattab is one of the more photogenic jihadi commanders. One frequently used image resembles that of the Argentinean revolutionary Ernesto "Che" Guevara (Figure 2-4). Shamil Basayev, the leader of the Chechen rebels who mentored Khattab in the 1990s, was a great admirer of Che Guevara. Whether Khattab actually sought to model his image on Che is unknown, but others have certainly suggested the possibility. Over time, the Russian press dubbed Khattab the "Arab Che Guevara."[10] The fact that a Marxist guerrilla leader emerged as a symbol of Western consumerism is ironic in and of itself. More puzzling is the fact that the same icon becomes a model for radical Islamists fighting the West. If anything, the case of Emir Khattab illustrates how the power of images may surpass that of political ideology in certain circumstances.

Figure 2-4. "The Sword of Islam (Khattab)."[11]

In all likelihood, Khattab's battlefield videos contributed to his iconic status among Islamist radicals. In fact, Khattab was one of the first jihadi commanders who brought cameramen into the field to document the Mujahideen's military activities. In the mid-1990s, Islamic charities, mosques, and religious bookstores across the Middle East, Europe, and the United States distributed VHS cassettes of the footage. Distribution of Khattab's battle videos occurred alongside footage of killed and mutilated Chechen women and children—atrocities allegedly carried out by Russian soldiers. Like Khattab's battlefield videos, these atrocity tapes initially attracted donors to the victims of the Second Chechen War. However, they also contributed to making Khattab himself an icon of the jihadi movement. The horrific images of suffering civilians—combined with images of Khattab's equally graphic revenge operations—reinforced the impression of Khattab's fighters as saviors of the Chechen people and, in a wider sense, defenders of Islam and Muslims.

The iconic status of *Hell of the Russians 2000* within the jihadi movement is evident in many later video productions of al-Qaeda and its affiliates. Allusions to the title "The Hell of X in Area X" have practically become a sub-genre within jihadi productions. *The Hell of the Americans in the Land of Khurasan* (Al-Qaeda in Afghanistan, 2005-present), *The Hell of the Apostates [in Algeria]* AQIM, 2005), and *The Hell of the Apostates in Somalia* (Al-Shabaab, 2009) are but a few examples. AQIM is perhaps the group that finds the most inspiration from *Hell of the Russians 2000*, as evidenced by the fact that they not only copy the title, but they also utilize the narrative framework and visual imagery of the original video series. For example, the image of burning vehicles (Figure 2-5) is a striking feature of *Hell of the Russians 2000*, which reappears in AQIM's *Lions of the East* from 2008.

Figure 2-5. Screen shots from *Hell of the Russians 2000* (left), and *Lions of the East* (right).

Other examples of iconic imagery found in both videos include footage of fighters pointing toward the sky as they walk to the battlefield indicating that they are on a "divine mission" and graphic images of dead enemies. We do not know whether scenes from *Hell of the Russians 2000* directly inspired those embedded in *Lions of the East*. Nevertheless, Khattab's *Hell of the Russians 2000* appears to have clearly established a pattern of iconic imagery that recurrently reappears in subsequent jihadi videos.

Given the improved production quality of AQIM's *The Raid of the Muezzin* from 2008 over *Hell of the Russians 2000*, some might presume that the former would attract more attention from the most radicalized members of the jihadist groups. After all, the technological advancements in the equipment available for making homemade videos since 2000 has been substantial, and the resulting production and editing capabilities are more professional. For example, AQIM has used two different camera crews that shot the attack from different camera angles. But in spite of their comparatively low production values, videos like *Hell of the Russians 2000* remain popular with captured jihadists. The next section discusses various possibilities for their continued popularity in more detail and presents a preliminary hypothesis about the "formula for success" of a jihadi video.

WHY DO SOME JIHADI VIDEOS BECOME ICONIC?

This section suggests that two factors comprise the formula for success of jihadi videos: namely, the timing of the video's release, and specific predictable combinations of visual imagery. These two hypotheses grew out of the previous analysis of the two jihadi videos most frequently mentioned in court cases: *Hell of the Russians 2000* and the USS *Cole* video (2001). Testing of the hypotheses on a larger dataset, however, will be necessary to assure their validity.

In order to explain why *Hell of the Russians 2000* became iconic, it is essential to look at the timing of the video's release. Khattab released *Hell of the Russians 2000* at the height of the Second Chechen War in 2000. As mentioned earlier, it was one of the first efforts by jihadists to make a video, which, in itself, probably contributed to its fame. Moreover, it contained images from an ongoing conflict widely known to Muslims living in Western countries at the time. Mosques and charities in both Europe and the United States were collecting money to aid Chechen refugees, and as part of that effort, such groups distributed pamphlets and screened videos illustrating the Muslim suffering in the conflict. The disturbing images helped the groups collect money, but also led to viewers feeling outraged, helpless and frustrated. Khattab's videos provided an outlet for these frustrations by showing that Muslims were capable of taking revenge. Moreover, the video motivated people to not only give money, but to identify with the Muslims in the videos and go fight themselves. Khattab's videos, in short, provided visual proof that any devoted Muslim could become a heroic fighter.

The second part of the formula for successful jihadi videos involves a predictable combination of visual images depicting "Muslim suffering" and "heroic fighters taking revenge." Al-Qaeda's first production, the USS *Cole* video from 2001, makes the associated pairings explicit. The video has a total length of about 2 hours and divides into two parts. The first 25 minutes shows images of Muslim suffering in various parts of the world, while a considerable amount of Part Two shows images of Muslim fighters training in Afghanistan. Released before September 11, 2001 (9/11) and the destruction of al-Qaeda's training camps in Afghanistan, the main purpose of the video was to encourage recruits to come to Afghanistan to train for "global jihad."

An important difference between *Hell of the Russians 2000* and the USS *Cole* video is that in the case of the USS *Cole* video, no immediate connection between those "suffering" (Muslims all over the world) and the object of revenge (a U.S. warship outside Yemen) exists. The Chechnya case is more straightforward, because footage shows Khattab attacking the same entity that allegedly carried out the atrocities on civilians. Al-Qaeda's media strategy seeks to overcome this challenge by emphasizing the use of images that presumably have a universal appeal to Muslim communities all over the world. The need for this universal appeal may explain why the USS *Cole* video includes many images from the Palestine-Israel conflict. While al-Qaeda has never had a strong presence in the Palestinian areas, they have repeatedly used images from that conflict as a universal symbol of "Western oppression of Muslims."

The timing of the USS *Cole* video's release is important for explaining that video's appeal for active jihadists. Issued a few months after the al-Aqsa intifada (also known as the "Second Palestinian Intifada") of 2000, it makes extensive use of footage from that conflict. Notably, it uses clips from the so-called Muhammad Dura video, which allegedly depicts a Palestinian boy shot by Israeli soldiers, while his father is trying to shield him from harm. Questions about the video's authenticity led to a 2007 French court ruling that the story presented in the video (i.e., that Israeli forces killed Mohammed al-Dura) was "not perfectly credible."[12] However, in the context of this analysis, the authenticity issue is not relevant. The important thing is that when al-Qaeda issued the USS *Cole* video, individuals in the Middle East and in the West regarded the clip as believable. As reported in the media, the al-Dura video "led to mass demonstrations against Israel and the Jews in the Western world."[13]

As-Sahab put great visual emphasis on al-Dura in the USS *Cole* video. In the video the image of the boy and his father repeatedly appears on the screen, each time with an audio track using the name "Muhammad" and a gunshot over emotional voices of preachers speaking about the injustice of the event.[14] As-Sahab's reference to "Muhammed" rather than "al-Dura" heightens the effect of the injustice, due to the association with the Prophet Muhammed and the boy's Muslim identity.

Al-Qaeda and its affiliates have used the al-Dura images in several of its subsequent productions, such as in *The Manhattan Raid* (*As-Sahab*, 2006) and *The Bouchaoui Attack* (*Groupe Salafiste pour la Prédication et le Combat*, 2007). The image's recurrent usage is an indication that the al-Dura image has become part of al-Qaeda's collection of iconic imagery.[15] The fact that the video's authenticity remains in dispute is a feature that future counter-messaging may exploit.

EXPLAINING THE ABSENCE OF "NEW" CONFLICT THEATERS

The success of early jihadi videos offer some hints about how certain videos become iconic in the context of online extremism. I argued previously that the videos' continued resonance might be due to timing of release and/or the paired association of certain types of visual images. Can this hypothesis explain the apparent lack of success of videos coming from Algeria and Somalia among jihadists in the West?

The hypothesis seems to hold true for videos coming from Iraq. These videos contain the two crucial types of images: "Muslim suffering and/or humiliation" combined with "heroic Muslims taking revenge." In the case of videos from the Iraqi conflict zone, plenty of footage of arrested radicals from the Abu Ghraib prison, for example, shows humiliation. Videos do not always contain images of mutilated women and children, perhaps because they may not have been as readily available as was the case in Chechnya and Bosnia. Instead, the fulfillment of the formal expectation of showing transgressions against Muslims occurs through images of heavily armed U.S. soldiers stepping on Iraqi soil. The emotional value of these appeals may not be quite as strong as that of the maimed bodies in Chechnya and Bosnia, but the images nevertheless communicate the feeling of humiliation.

In the videos from the Iraqi conflict zone, the "revenge" images are again explicit. For example, two of the 18 court cases mention the Islamic Army of Iraq's well-known *Juba the Baghdad Sniper* (2006). In one of those cases, the reference occurs using admiring terms. The *Juba the Baghdad Sniper* video differs from others from Iraq in that the footage is especially dramatic. It shows a series of sniper attacks on U.S. soldiers, often with minimal distance between the cameraman and the victim (see Figure 2-6). The close-up positions the viewer as a virtual participant in the video's scenario. As a result the footage depicts a clear and explicit "revenge" on the "foreign occupier." This revenge element was important for the Iraqi resistance movement at a time when sectarian war and indiscriminate attacks on civilians had begun to discredit the movement's legitimacy.

Figure 2-6. Screen Grab from *Juba*.

Jihadi videos from both Algeria and Somalia lack images of an explicit "foreign occupier." In the case of both conflict zones, the jihadi groups are fighting their own governments. AQIM portrays the Algerian police as the enemy, but the visual effect is not nearly as striking as when the enemy image is that of an American soldier. While the release dates of the videos appear strategic, the Algerian and Somali conflicts lack strong visual images of Muslims who suffer at the hands of a "foreign aggressor." Indeed, those Muslims who are suffering may be suffering at the hands of fellow Muslims.

The discussion about how jihadi videos portray various conflict theaters deserves further exploration. For example, do the jihadi groups in areas such as Algeria, Somalia, and Afghanistan continue to use iconic images associated with al-Qaeda to attract supporters, or do they seek to develop their own iconic visual symbols? What is the effect of such symbols on potential recruits? While the questions are beyond the scope of this chapter, the Afghan Taliban today use images that are radically different from those the insurgents in Iraq use. One example is the way the groups present Western hostages on tape. In 2004, AQI filmed the U.S. hostage Nick Berg wearing an orange jumpsuit (similar to those used in the Guantanamo Bay prison) and sitting in front of an execution squad. Indeed, the video also depicted the execution itself. In 2009, the Taliban in Afghanistan issued a video of their hostage, Bowe Bergdahl, wearing local attire and digging into a generous meal. Ample reasons exist to believe that al-Qaeda and its affiliates are conscious about what visual symbols they are using to maximize the effect of their propaganda videos, which makes it all the more important to identify and study these symbols.

CONCLUSION AND POLICY IMPLICATIONS

This preliminary analysis shows that gathering data from court cases is a fruitful approach for studying the effect of visual images in radicalization. So far, the most surprising finding from such an approach is that the earliest jihadi videos—especially those from Chechnya—seem to have magnified status within the jihadi community in spite of their relatively low technical sophistication. Had this analysis relied instead on the "most viewed" videos on jihadi Internet forums as the basis of its statistical analysis, such a finding would have remained hidden from view.

This chapter hypothesizes that associations of certain visual images are important for the success of jihadi video in reaching active jihadists. Images depicting "Muslim suffering" and "heroic fighters taking revenge" make a potentially powerful mixture. Videos such as *Hell of the Russians 2000* and *Juba the Baghdad Sniper* logically connect the "oppressor" with the "target of revenge." Absent the presence of such a logical connection, well-known issues with universal appeal—such as the "occupation" of Palestine by Israel—become the main visual icons. As this analysis demonstrates, the al-Qaeda network has used this media strategy since As-Sahab issued its very first video in 2001.

Yet, there remains surprisingly little research on the role of iconic images in jihadi videos. Rather than studying "jihadi video genres," future studies should focus on identifying iconic images in jihadi propaganda films and hypothesize about their causal effects based on data from real-life cases. Another topic worth exploring is how the use of iconic images changes over time and across geographical areas. This analysis provides a necessary first step toward developing effective strategies to counter al-Qaeda's visual messaging.

ENDNOTES - CHAPTER 2

1. A "jihadi video" is a video produced by a jihadi group, or supporters of jihadi groups, for propaganda purposes. A "Jihadi group" is a militant Islamist group which supports al-Qaeda's ideology. They do not include nationalist groups such as Hezbollah and Hamas.

2. There are some exceptions, such as analyses of how randomly selected, Muslim audiences in Great Britain receive jihadi videos and of how YouTube users received them. See Paul Baines *et al.*, "Muslim Voices: The British Muslim Response to Islamic Video-Polemic—An Exploratory Study," Cranfield School of Management Research Paper Series, Research Paper No. 3/06, Bedford, UK: December 2006, pp. 1-28; Maura Conway and Lisa McInerney, "Jihadi Video & Auto-radicalisation: Evidence from an Exploratory YouTube Study," paper presented at the "EuroISI 2008, "First European Conference on Intelligence and Security Informatics," Esbjerg, Denmark, December 3–5, 2008.

3. Films of the same genre tend to present the same type of narrative and employ a standard set of visual symbols. "Operational films" contain symbols of masculinity, comradeship and adventure, while "Martyr films" often send a poignant message of self-sacrifice and divine rewards. Films produced by al-Qaeda and its affiliates follow a standard set of "genre conventions" that have stayed relatively constant over time. Short films such as "decapitation videos" or "roadside bomb explosions" usually contain one visual symbol, but other films combine multiple visual symbols. As-Sahab typically combines images of Muslim suffering, corrupt Arab leaders and heroic al-Qaeda fighters to present its grand narrative that the Muslim world is under attack by the West, that al-Qaeda is an effective group willing to stand up against it, and that it is the religious duty of every Muslim to join the fight.

4. Thus, for example, in the case of the Glasgow airport bombers, Mohammed Asha was the person who owned the computer

where most jihadi videos were found. Yet he was later found not guilty and acquitted of all charges.

5. Thomas Hegghammer, "Global Jihadism After the Iraq War," *Middle East Journal*, Vol. 60, No. 1, Winter 2006, pp. 20-21.

6. Michael Ignatieff, "The Terrorist as Auteur," *New York Times*, November 14, 2004, available from *www.nytimes.com/2004/11/14/ movies/14TERROR.html*.

7. "Zawahiri's Letter to Zarqawi (English Translation)," available from *www.ctc.usma.edu/posts/zawahiris-letter-to-zarqawi-english-translation-2*.

8. The webpage appeared in 2009 and in June 2009 the archive contained some 2,500 jihadi videos and audiotapes produced between 1979-2009, available from Arshif al-jihad, *www. jarchive.info*.

9. Osama bin Laden established As-Sahab, now considered the al-Qaeda leadership's official mouthpiece, around 2000.

10. Brian Glyn Williams, "Operation Enduring Freedom 2001-2005: Waging Counter-Jihad in Post-Taliban Central Eurasia," paper presented at the 46th Annual International Studies Association Convention, Waikiki, Hawaii, March 2005, p.18.

11. "Tasmim jadid bi-'unwan sayf al-islam (khattab)" ("New Design Entitled The Sword of Islam [Khattab]"), available from *www.muslm.net/vb/showthread.php?329498*.

12. "Al-Durra Case Revisited," *Wall Street Journal*, May 27, 2008, available from *online.wsj.com/news/articles/SB12118 3757337520921*.

13. Richard Landes, "The Muhammad Al-Dura Blood Libel: A Case Analysis," New York: Jewish Council for Public Affairs, available from *www.jcpa.org/article/the-muhammad-al-dura-blood-libel- a-case-analysis-2/*.

14. *The Destruction of the Destroyer* USS *Cole, Part 1,* film No. 647, Jihadist Video Database, Kjeller, Norway: Norwegian Defence Research Establishment, accessed on September 25, 2012, 15:36 - 16:20.

15. *The Manhattan Raid, Part 1* and *The Bouchaoui Attack,* films No. 326 and 498, Jihadist Video Database, Kjeller, Norway: Norwegian Defence Research Establishment, accessed on September 25, 2012.

CHAPTER 3

VISUAL RECONCILIATION AS STRATEGY OF RESPONSE TO OFFENDING IMAGES ONLINE

Carol K. Winkler

Images posted online of American soldiers "mugging" with enemy corpses, urinating on dead members of the Taliban, and posing in front of symbols reminiscent of Nazi swastikas in 2012 illustrate the power of the Internet to widely and efficiently distribute offending videos and photographs to online audiences. The anonymously posted video with the tag, "Scout sniper team 4 with 3rd battalion 2nd marines out of camp lejuene peeing on dead talibans," alone generated more than 20,000 follow-on posts garnering tens of millions of views within 4 months of its initial January 11, 2012, YouTube appearance.[1] In response, then Secretary of Defense Leon Panetta warned an Army brigade at Fort Benning, GA, that such images, "can put your fellow service members at risk. They can hurt morale. They can damage our standing in the world, and they can cost lives."[2]

Besides inflaming anti-U.S. sentiment and violent acts of retribution within the current military deployments, offending photographs and videos have even more propaganda value for violent extremist groups because they can be co-opted and used at a later time. When re-circulated across time and place in the online environment, such images do more than simply prompt recall of past bad acts by members of the U.S. military now operating in Afghanistan or other theaters; they also function as de-contextualized re-enactments of the offending behaviors. Future viewers can witness the affronts online repeatedly with less understanding of the mitigating factors present at the time of the initial offending behaviors. As a result, offending images function as a ready cache of material available for violent extremist groups to support their future propaganda claims.

Previous scholarly examinations of the strategies available for handling public accusations of offending conduct have focused exclusively on verbal, discursive approaches. Most notable amongst these efforts are B. L. Ware and Wil A. Linkugel's seminal essay outlining a four-part taxonomy of the generic argumentative strategies available for speakers delivering apologies (denial, bolstering, differentiation, and transcendence), and Benoit's identification of five strategies appropriate for self-defense (denial, evasion of responsibility, reduction of the offensiveness of the act, the promise of corrective action, and mortification).[3] More recently, scholars have concentrated on situational factors that offer a more nuanced understanding of appropriate verbal response strategies. They have focused on the level of guilt of the accused, the nature of the accusation (i.e., whether lodged against policies or character), and variations in eastern and western audiences' cultural expectations as key contextual factors needing attention for effective national apologies.[4]

None of this earlier research, however, examines the *visual* strategies needed for responding to offending images in the online environment. Such an oversight is unfortunate, as images do serve as powerful sources of both verbal and visual argumentative claims.[5] A commonly cited example demonstrating the impact of visual argument involves the video *Silent Scream*, produced in support of the U.S. anti-abortion movement.

Responding to the abortion rights advocates' recurrent argument that fetuses were not yet human beings, the producers of *Silent Scream* displayed disturbing sonogram footage that purportedly showed a fetus screaming during its own abortion.[6] While members of the pro-life movement had previously insisted that life began at the point of conception, the video footage in *Silent Scream* added a persuasive visual argument for undecided audience members: namely, that a fetus was human and felt pain from the abortion procedure.

This chapter will help fill in the research gap by offering insights into the development of a specifically visual strategy for responding to offending images online. First, it will narrow the field of offending images that warrant a visual response by identifying factors associated with an image's resonant audience appeal across time and place. Based upon an analysis of images associated with historical national apologies from leaders around the globe, it will then offer visual reconciliation as the most appropriate response strategy.

IMAGES THAT WARRANT VISUAL RESPONSE

The number of potentially offending images available for incorporation into extremists' propaganda is vast, in part because editing capabilities can alter the verbal or visual context of pictures and video so easily. Accordingly, the first step needed for any strategic visual response plan is to narrow the field to the key set of images likely to retain currency with online viewers across space and time. Many images have an initial, flash appeal for viewers, but most fade away without a noticeable, lasting impact in the online environment. Responding to all offending images would stretch resources thin and, indeed, if an image is about to fade from public memory, insistently responding to it could well sustain and prolong its impact. However, certain images do sustain their resonance with target audiences, thereby elevating the need for an effective response. As this chapter argues in the following pages such lasting images include those that incorporate the subjunctive voice, contribute to argumentative convergence, and function as political identity markers.

Subjunctive Voice.

One of the most extensive published studies of image re-circulation to date is Barbie Zelizer's *About to Die: How News Images Move the American Public.*[7] Zelizer identifies historical news images that have continued to circulate in American newspaper and television media outlets long past the moment when they first appeared. She concludes that the subjunctive voice, a concept borrowed from linguistics, explains why certain images continue to resonate with American audiences. She begins by drawing a distinction between images that merely document "what is" from those that employ the subjunctive voice, i.e., those that raise notions of "as if" or "what could or should be."[8] She identifies three recurrent characteristics of the subjunctive voice: contingency, imagination, and emotion. Contingency means that the interpretation of images can change over time, making their meaning adaptive to future circumstances. Imagination functions in response to the ambiguous meaning of images by opening opportunities for viewers to fill in the moments before and after the frozen frame. Finally, "as-if" images prompt unpredictable emotional responses based on how the viewer fills in the context of the frozen image. Zelizer insists that, at least for a small group of images that employ the subjective voice, the public and press alike should consider the widespread characterizations of photojournalistic practice as objective and dispassionate as misguided.

One image that illustrates the use of subjunctive voice is the widely circulated photograph of the hooded man standing on a box with electrical cords attached to his hands at Abu Ghraib prison. The meaning of the image is contingent, as some consider the photograph to be clear evidence of U.S. torture of Iraqi civilians, but others view it as proof of the U.S. commander's lack of control at the prison. Viewers' imaginations fill in whether the man had participated in acts of terrorism prior to his placement on the box, whether he subsequently endured electrocution, whether he tired to the point of falling from the box, or whether he died. Emotional reactions to the image include, for example, horror, glee, satisfaction, discomfort, or anger, depending on how viewers fill in the events before and after the frozen frame. The photograph's evident reliance on subjunctive voice portends that it will continue to circulate in the online environment for years to come.

Argumentative Convergence.

A second factor predictive of which offending images are likely to continue circulating in the online environment is convergence. Argumentation theorists Chaim Perelman and Lucie Olbrechts-Tyteca explain why convergence magnifies the argumentative potential of individual claims when they write:

> . . . If several distinct arguments lead to a single con-
> clusion, be it general or partial, final or provisional, the
> value attributed to the conclusion and to each separate
> argument will be augmented, for the likelihood that
> several entirely erroneous arguments would reach the
> same conclusion is very small.[9]

In the visual realm, argumentative convergence can either occur within the context of a single image (i.e., when the substance and the compositional elements reinforce the same argumentative claim) or when a visual argument combines with other visual, textual, or aural arguments to lead the audience to draw the same conclusion.

One widely circulated image snapped at the start of the U.S. war in Iraq in 2003 illustrates the point. The photograph shows Ali Abbas, a 12-year-old boy burned and maimed when U.S. bombs hit his Bagh-dad home on the first day of the Iraq War.[10] On a substantive level, the iconic image provides evidence for the claim that U.S. military attacks harm innocent civilians. The compositional elements of the photo-graph reinforce the claim by contributing to argumen-tative convergence in ways other images of the war's civilian casualties do not. The close-up framing of the photographed body positions Abbas looking directly at the viewer from an intimate distance. The stance, coupled with his head in the lower left quadrant of the screen, takes on a poignant meaning as it mim-ics that of an infant in the natural pose for breastfeed-ing. Abbas' bandaged, amputated arms in the photo bolster such an interpretation, as, like a newborn, his head is now disproportionately larger than his other shown body parts. The handle of Ali's stretcher re-sembles that of an infant carrier, and the hand enter-ing the frame from the top left corner is suggestive of a caretaker's hand preparing to wipe the drool from an infant's face. Together, the compositional elements converge with the substance of the photo to argue that U.S. actions harm the most vulnerable members of the Muslim community.

The Abbas photograph further contributes to argumentative convergence through its frequent paired association with other offending iconic images. One such pairing, appearing in al-Qaeda's videos recently, joins the Abbas photograph with an image of another 12-year-old boy, Mohammed al-Dura, filmed by Talal abu Rahmah for France2.[11] The circulating frozen frame extracted from the France2 video footage shows al-Dura, a scared boy crouching behind his father during an Israeli Defense Forces-Palestinian gun battle. Later in the videotape, the boy lies across his father's lap allegedly killed by Israeli forces, according to the original story that France2 broadcast. While French courts have adjudicated whether the France2 story produced a true or staged account of the al-Dura incident, the image, nevertheless, has come to symbolize the Second Intifada for many in the Middle East. The quick cut between the Abbas and al-Dura images visually invites the inference that a terrorist conspiracy exists between the United States and Israel to target Muslim populations, as the actions of both nations' militaries appear to harm young Muslim civilians unable to defend themselves or to fight back in any way.

Political Identity Markers.

A third factor contributing to the re-circulation of images across time and space is their ability to function as cultural identifiers. Janis Edwards and Carol K. Winkler maintain that members of the political elite and the rank-and-file citizenry alike widely recognize a small subset of images with adaptive, flexible meanings as readily identifiable, political markers of culture.[12] Robert Hariman and John Lucaites agree, maintaining that specific iconic images that avoid rigid interpretation or meaning, "can foster social connectedness, political identity, and cultural continuity."[13] By transcending particularized meanings embedded in specific contexts, such images do not lose their resilience and currency over time. Instead, they come to function as identifying markers of the cultures in which they circulate.

Communication scholars have identified five sources of rhetorical power that intersect to create political markers of a culture. These include the ability to reproduce ideology, to communicate social knowledge, to shape collective memory, to model citizenship, and to become the figural resources for communicative action.[14] Examples of photographs of individuals that have become positive indicators of collective identity for the American culture include Joe Rosenthal's Iwo Jima photograph, Dorethea Lange's "Migrant Mother," and Alfred Eisenstaedt's Time Square "Kiss on V-E Day." Markers of political culture, however, can also evoke negative emotions, such as Nick Ut's "Accidental Napalm" photograph from the Vietnam War. Once an image emerges as a political marker demarcating who belongs and who falls outside of the culture, expansions and contractions of the images' meaning over time become revealing about shifts in cultural definitions.[15]

In sum, once offending images that employ the subjunctive voice, participate in argumentative conversion, and/or function as political markers of the culture begin to circulate in the online environment, response images should become an important component of the counter-messaging strategy. The need to deploy a visual, rather than just verbal, response strategy emerges from the unique power of visual images outlined in Chapter 1 of this volume. The visual response, however, should go beyond simple identification and posting of images that share the qualities enumerated previously in an effort to facilitate the response's re-circulation. As the next section will detail, a visual approach of reconciliation should serve as the strategic framework for responding to offending images in the online environment.

RECONCILIATION AS VISUAL RESPONSE STRATEGY

Scholars who have examined how national leaders historically craft public speeches in response to accusations of offensive words or deeds conclude that such officials generally rely upon one of two recurrent strategic approaches. The first of these is apologia, which William Benoit and Susan Brinson define as, "a recurring type of discourse designed to restore face, image, or reputation after an alleged or suspected wrongdoing," that occurs during many apologies.[16] The second is reconciliation, which John Hatch defines as, "a dialogic rhetorical process of healing between the parties."[17] Based on an examination of visual images of national apologies delivered around the globe over the past 4 decades, I will argue that, of the two strategic approaches, images associated with reconciliation have more lasting circulation in the online environment. As offending online images serve as a reminder, if not an ongoing affront, to certain audiences across time and space, the process of visual reconciliation emerges as the preferable strategic response.

The following sections explore four key differences between reconciliation and apologia, as well as demonstrate how images of reconciliation have sustained currency for all viewers. To avoid any confusion, my use of the term "apology" will mean the tactical use of actual words and images within specific situations to express regret and remorse for prior offending acts without regard for the speakers' strategic choices. I will simultaneously follow the lead of the previously referenced scholars and employ the term "apologia" strategically as, "A recurring type of discourse designed to restore face, image, or reputation after an alleged or suspected wrongdoing," that occurs during many apologies. The endnotes accompanying this section provide the online addresses (URLs) for each of the referenced images.

Forgiveness versus Face-Saving.

One distinguishing feature between apologia and reconciliation involves the desired goal the speaker intends to achieve with the audience. Speakers using apologia strive to restore their own credibility and remove any perception they might be guilty of involvement in the transgression.[18] Speakers seeking reconciliation are interested in restoring dialogue, instead of pursuing the purposes of shifting blame, denying charges, or some other form of blame avoidance or image repair.[19] The dialogue function of reconciliation affords the injured party an ongoing opportunity to either accept or refuse to accept the offered apology, or even to accept, but still demand future apologies in the interests of restorative, rather than punitive, justice.

The most frequent visual strategy deployed in images of national apologies involves a headshot of a designated national leader or other representative apologizing for inappropriate words or deeds before a television camera. The approach, frequently accompanied by a speaker's face-saving verbal appeals, rarely results in an image that has lasting circulation in the online environment. An exclusive use of a headshot visually removes the option of reconciliation, as the approach crops out one party in the dialogue. For example, the January 12, 2012, headshot of U.S. Secretary of State Hillary Clinton speaking from behind a podium as she condemned video images of Marines pictured desecrating dead members of the Taliban illustrates the point. The head-shot positions her as speaking to all television viewers without designating who has the right to accept her words or who can demand more from the United States by way of continued apologies.[20]

By contrast, circulating images clipped from the February 24, 2012, news video of Acting Assistant Secretary of Defense Peter Lavoy apologizing for U.S. military members burning Qu'rans provides visual documentation that the U.S. Government sought reconciliation with members of the Muslim community.[21] The physical site of the apology was the All Dulles Area Muslim Society, one of the largest mosques in the United States. The location, evident in each frozen frame of the event on the Internet, documents that aggrieved Muslims are willing to listen to the apology by the U.S. military leader. The backs of individual congregation members' heads, coupled with Imam Mohamed Magid flanking Assistant Secretary Lavoy and nodding at times during his apology, provide visual evidence that some Muslims wish to continue the dialogue with the United States, rather than reject the appeal outright and pursue more violent responses. Further, Assistant Secretary Lavoy's public vulnerability, whereby his apology might have elicited a negative reaction from the congregation, the Imam, or both, helps elevate the stature of the Muslim members of his dialogue in accordance with the norms of reconciliation. While the image of Assistant Secretary Lavoy's apology is unlikely to reach as many viewers as the offending image of the burned Qu'rans, it nevertheless remains available for those wishing to moderate anger over the incident in future contexts by documenting the U.S. military's efforts at reconciliation with the Muslim community.

Images can also function as arguments for reconciliation even when those apologizing do not speak directly to those aggrieved. On June 15, 2010, for example, British Prime Minister David Cameron apologized before the House of Commons for the 1972 Bloody Sunday killings, where British authorities killed 14 unarmed protesters who had criticized the British government for detaining suspected IRA terrorists without trial.[22] The most widely re-circulated image of the event, however, does not occur inside the House of Commons chamber at the Palace of Westminster itself; instead, it is a still image captured from the video of the families and friends of the dead outside the chamber, who had come to London to pronounce publicly the innocence of those the British government had killed, as they watched the speech. The still image of the audience, cheering in response to Prime Minister Cameron's apology, supports the conclusion that the British government was making progress in reconciling with the injured parties for the slain members of their community.

Reflection versus Preservation.

Besides having distinctive goals for their audiences, speakers delivering national apologies have differential goals for themselves based on whether they seek to employ apologia or reconciliation. Speakers relying on apologia are not striving to change themselves; instead, they speak in defense of themselves to order to change the perceptions of others.[23] Speakers attempting to reconcile with aggrieved parties, by contrast, focus on self-reflection as a necessary step for preventing the offense from recurring in the future.[24] The process of self-reflection, if genuinely and properly implemented, helps restore the dignity of those injured by the previous bad acts. The circulating online images examined here provide evidence that the leaders are engaging in moments of self-reflection consistent with the goal of reconciliation. In rare cases, moments of self-reflection can even serve as the complete argument, shedding any need for an accompanying speech of apology.

The image most known for demonstrating self-reflection at moments of national apology involves West German Chancellor Willy Brandt visiting a Jewish war memorial in a Warsaw ghetto on December 7, 1970.[25] Chancellor Brandt's state visit to Warsaw was an attempt to improve relations with Poland and the Soviet Union, with a planned side trip to commemorate the victims of the Warsaw Ghetto uprising of 1943. Overcome by emotion as he approached the memorial, Brandt fell to his knees in an act of repentance. He offered no words of apology. Later, he would explain:

I had to do something to express the particularity of the commemoration at the ghetto monument. On the abyss of German history and carrying the burden of the millions who were murdered, I did what people do when words fail them.[26]

A virtual consensus of academic studies and related press coverage of the incident consider the image of Chancellor Brandt's powerful act of self-reflection on the past wrong acts of Germany as iconic.

Brandt's image, however, is far from alone as a photographed act of self-reflection during times of national apology. At times, such images focus on leaders surveying the consequences of their own prior acts, as when Russian President Vladamir Putin made a hospital visit to some of the 100 hostage casualties caused by his October 23, 2002, order to gas the Dubrovka Theater that Chechen separatists had held.[27] Reconciliation images also document leaders examining the prior bad acts of their predecessors, as a photograph of U.S. President George W. Bush and First Lady Laura Bush during their visit to Goree Island off the coast of Senegal, a symbol of the West African slave trade, illustrates.[28] While President Bush did not formally apologize during his trip, he did call slavery "one of the greatest crimes of history." The archetypal image of the President and First Lady moving both literally and figuratively through the darkness into the light as they walk through the slave quarters makes the visual argument that the President is engaging in the process of self-reflection.

Other re-circulated images of national apology infer that the offender has already reflected, recognized wrongdoing, and chosen to take some redemptive action. One example involves the image of the United

States flying its embassy flag at half-mast during U.S. Ambassador Thomas Pickering's trip to apologize to the Chinese in response to an incident where a B-2 bomber mistakenly struck the Chinese Embassy in Belgrade on May 7, 1999, killing three Chinese journalists and injuring more than 20 others.[29] A photograph of Argentine President Nestor Kirchner removing the official portraits of military leaders who, during the junta's 7-year reign, killed more than 30,000 people considered sympathetic to the communists' message, offers another example of redemption sought after many steps of the process of self-reflection.[30]

Images of self-reflection during national apologies can employ a range of representatives to disavow wrongful acts of the past. Most frequently, the photographed spokesperson is a head of state or some other organizational leader responsible for those who committed the offending act. U.S. Marine Corps General John Allen, for example, publicly apologized in his full dress uniform to the Afghan President, government, and people for the burning of the Qu'rans that occurred under his personal command of the International Security Force in Afghanistan.[31] Images of community leaders participating in public processes of self-reflection can also help heighten the call for contemplation to prevent future harmful acts. One notable image of community leaders, snapped at the interfaith vigil in the National Cathedral after the attacks of September 11, 2001, displayed religious leaders dressed to display many faiths sitting together in hopes of moving toward a better future built on mercy, rather than further violent acts by individuals in the name of religion.[32] Finally, images of self-reflection by rank-and-file community members can also facilitate the goals of reconciliation, as when 250,000 Australians crossed the Sydney Bridge to symbolize their denunciation of their nation's prior bad acts against that nation's aborigines. The image's inclusion of the word "SORRY," displayed in skywriting above the bridge, creates an iconic reminder of the outcome of Australia's nonaboriginal citizens' process of self-reflection.[33]

Open versus Closed Argument.

A third key distinction between apologia and reconciliation deals with the process associated with issuing national apologies. Apologia is an argumentative form that seeks closure or, put another way, conflict resolution for past acts of wrongdoing. Those who apologize strive to inhibit future discourse about their transgressions and to move on to other matters.[34] Reconciliation, by contrast, is a long-term process of restoring dignity to the wronged party. Those participating in attempts at reconciliation show a continued willingness to engage in dialogue that recalls memories of the past and that recognizes both the differences and differential power between the two parties involved in the dispute.[35] A number of online images of national apology demonstrate that some transgressors do treat the recovery process from their past misdeeds as an ongoing process.

The most obvious example was a photograph of the grounds outside the Parliament Building of Australia when Prime Minister Kevin Rudd apologized for offenses against the aboriginal peoples of Australia.[36] During the nation's history, the Australian government's bad acts included permitting aboriginal children to be put up for adoption to white families in hopes of "breeding out their color." Prime Minister Rudd issued the national apology only after the country's state parliaments, churches, and social welfare agencies had first apologized. The image of "SORRY. THE FIRST STEP" written on the Parliament lawn makes the visual argument that Australia's apologies were only an initial step in the dialogue, with an open invitation for further steps to help remedy the historical offenses against the nation's aborigines.

Another example of an image of national apology that argues for a future, open dialogue is the photograph of U.S. President Bill Clinton snapped when he visited Ugandan school children at Kisowera School of Mukono in 1998. President Clinton did not officially apologize for slavery at the site but did tell the children that, "European Americans received the fruits of the slave trade and we were wrong in that"[37] and promised 120 million dollars in educational improvements as a form of reparations. The image places the focus on reconciliation for the future, as the President joins hands with the school children, Uganda's future.[38] It also recalls the memory of the U.S. history with slavery by staging a reenactment of the compositional elements of a remarkably similar photograph, one that captured an image of then President Abraham Lincoln, who had hopes for future reconciliation as he walked through the streets of Richmond, VA, at the end of the American Civil War.[39] Clinton, like Lincoln, towered over the children as he walked hand-in-hand with them; adults flanked both sides of the two leaders as they moved forward.

Long-term Reunion versus Short-term Gain.

A final distinction between apologia and reconciliation relates to the desired outcomes from the transgressor's response. Apologia focuses on short-term gains achievable by regaining favor with audiences already predisposed to the speaker's arguments.[40] Reconciliation, by contrast, has a goal of understanding the long-term processes of image restoration and mutual respect between the aggrieved and the transgressor. Attempts at credible reconciliation utilize symbols of reunion to demonstrate that the aggrieved has *genuinely* granted the forgiveness sought by the offender.[41] Visual images freeze the moment of genuine forgiveness and, when replayed in the online environment, carry forward the steps of reunification into perpetuity.

The most common symbol of reunion following a national apology is the handshake, denoting respect between the two parties. Accompanying facial expressions, such as smiles and direct eye contact, contribute to the handshake image's ability to argue that sincere forgiveness has occurred. At times, the demographic characteristics of the participants shaking hands become reinforcing evidence for the authenticity of the reconciliation attempt. After former South African President William De Klerk apologized for 4 decades of rule by his nation's white supremacist government, for example, the stark contrast between the skin tones of President De Klerk and Bishop Desmond Tutu, then acting in his role as Secretary General of the South African Council of Churches, makes a visual argument for the reunion of the races, the goal strived for during the proceedings of South Africa's Truth and Reconciliation commissions.[42]

Besides the handshake, the use of physical space in images associated with national apologies can argue for genuine reunion between the transgressor and the aggrieved. Consider the widely circulated image of President Clinton and Mr. Herman Shaw, one of the few remaining survivors of the Tuskegee Syphilis study. The photographers snapped the picture after Clinton apologized to the survivors, family members, children, and grandchildren of those the U.S. Government had told were receiving treatment for syphilis, but instead denied them treatment after failing to obtain their consent to participate in the study. The Clinton-Shaw image records such a close personal distance between the two men that, even though Mr. Shaw does not look directly at President Clinton, his acceptance of the apology appears genuine.[43]

Other compositional elements of photographs can also contribute to the perception of a genuine, successful reconciliation. An image of a meeting between President Barack Obama, Vice President Joseph Biden, Harvard Professor Henry Gates, and Sergeant Joseph Crowley illustrates a number of other visual strategies available to signal that genuine reconciliation has occurred. Prior to the meeting President Obama had announced that Sergeant Crowley "acted stupidly" when he arrested Gates during his response to a call about an alleged burglary attempt at Gates' home. Physical presence and setting, seating arrangements, props, and dress that the photographer captured in the image all invite the audience to infer that the previous conflict between the men was in the past. The image documents that each of the men agreed to be present at the informal meeting on the White House lawn. The alternating seating of the black and white participants visually responds to the underlying charge of racism that magnified the arrest into a national news story. The beers and the willingness of the nation's two top leaders to remove their suit jackets reinforce the conclusion that the men share an informal camaraderie. Together, the image functions as visual evidence that the men have moved past the incident and forgiven each other for the misunderstanding.[44] Those familiar with the events leading up to beer-gate (as the U.S. media dubbed the encounter) might consider the image staged and thus lacking in the sincerity and genuineness required for reconciliation. However, just as aspects of the context associated with offending images drop away through re-circulation in the online environment, the compositional elements of apparent genuine reconciliation will continue to exist long after the photograph's staging is forgotten.

CONCLUDING REMARKS

Not all offending images circulating in the online environment warrant a visual response or even an apology by national leaders. Nevertheless, failure to respond to the small number of potent images of transgressions that share characteristics qualifying them for continued recirculation in future propaganda efforts could be a costly mistake. Visual responses to offending images need to fit within a strategic framework in an effort to send a consistent, coherent message to online viewers. Reconciliation provides a fruitful choice, as its long-term goals match the ongoing need to handle ever-circulating images that offend.

Future examinations of visual response strategies to offending images should also focus on the most efficient method of response delivery to the targeted audience. Recently, the military community has posted numerous videos documenting high-ranking officers, without the benefit of protective gear or weapons, apologizing for the recent rash of offending images to small groups of citizens of Afghanistan. These messages clearly comply with a key strategic goal of reconciliation, i.e., to position the transgressor as both open and vulnerable to the reaction of the aggrieved. Viewership of that message, however, has limits, because to retrieve the videos from YouTube, potential audience members must know the "dvids" access code for the military's responses. The response videos of the military are difficult to find under more common, English vernacular search engine terms for YouTube, such as "peeing marines," "burned Qu'rans," etc. The people who know how to find these videos, in other words, are the ones who probably already know they exist and do not need to search for them. While devising the most cost-beneficial approach of message delivery to target audiences is beyond the goal of this chapter, an effective, visual response strategy certainly requires that viewers can easily access any response messages.

ENDNOTES - CHAPTER 3

1. Cited image of Anonymous, "Scout sniper team 4 with 3rd battalion 2nd marines out of camp lejuene peeing on dead talibans," available from *www.youtube.com/watch?v=ui O1C6JzBbc.*

2. "Defense Secretary Leon Panetta Warns Troops About Misconduct," *Los Angeles Times,* May 4, 2012, available from *www. articles.latimes.com/2012/may/04/nation/la-na-panetta-troops-20120505.*

3. B. L. Ware and Wil A. Linkugel, "They Spoke in Defense of Themselves: On the Generic Criticism of Apologia," *Quarterly Journal of Speech,* Vol. 59, No. 3, October 1973, pp. 273-283; William L. Benoit, *Accounts, Excuses and Apologies: A Theory of Image Restoration Strategies.* Albany, NY: State University of New York Press, 1995.

4. See Joy Koesten and Robert C. Rowland, "The Rhetoric of Atonement," *Communication Studies,* Vol. 55, No. 1, Spring 2004, pp. 68-88; Halford Ross Ryan, "*Kategoria* and *Apologia:* On Their

Rhetorical Criticism as a Speech Act," *Quarterly Journal of Speech,* Vol. 68, No. 3, August 1982, pp. 254-261; Takeshi Suzuki and Frans H. van Eemeren, "'This Painful Chapter': An Analysis of Emperor Akihito's Apologia in the Context of Dutch Old Sores," *Argumentation and Advocacy,* Vol. 41, No. 2, Fall 2004, pp. 102-111.

5. Argumentation scholars have concluded that visual images function as data or reasoning in support of claims, as well as claims on their own. For a review of related literature, see Catherine Palczewski, "Argument in the Off-Key," G. Thomas Goodnight, ed., *Arguing Communication and Culture,* Vol. 1, Washington, DC: National Communication Association, 2002, pp. 1-23.

6. See, for example, Robert J. Branham, "The Role of the Convert in *Eclipse of Reason* and *The Silent Scream,*" *Quarterly Journal of Speech,* Vol. 77, No. 4, November 1991, pp. 407-426.

7. Barbie Zelizer, *About to Die: How News Images Move the American Public,* New York: Oxford University Press, 2010.

8. *Ibid.,* p. 14.

9. Chaim Perelman and Lucie Olbrechts-Tyteca, *The New Rhetoric: A Treatise on Argumentation.* Notre Dame, IN: Notre Dame University Press, 1969, p. 741.

10. Cited image of Ali Abbas, available from *www.habibtoumi. com/2010/01/20/kuwait-mp-lashes-out-at-government-funding-for-iraq-hospital/ali-abbas/.*

11. Cited image of Mohammed al-Dura, available from *news. bbc.co.uk/2/hi/middle_east/952600.stm.*

12. Janis L. Edwards and Carol K. Winkler, "Representative Form and the Visual Ideograph: The Iwo Jima Image and Editorial Cartoons," *Quarterly Journal of Speech,* Vol. 83, No. 3, August 1997, pp. 289-310.

13. Robert Hariman and John L. Lucaites, *No Caption Needed: Iconic Photographs, Public Culture, and Liberal Democracy,* Chicago, IL: University of Chicago Press, 2007, p. 111.

14. *Ibid.*, pp. 25-47.

15. Carol K. Winkler, *In the Name of Terrorism: Presidents on Political Violence in the Post-World War II Era,* Albany, NY: State University of New York Press, 2006.

16. William L. Benoit and Susan L. Brinson, "AT&T: 'Apologies are Not Enough'," *Communication Quarterly,* Vol. 2, No. 1, Winter 1994, p. 75.

17. John B. Hatch, "Beyond *Apologia*: Racial Reconciliation and Apologies for Slavery," *Western Journal of Communication,* Vol. 70, No. 3, July 2006, p. 187.

18. Kevin E. McClearey, "Audience Effects of Apologia," *Communication Quarterly,* Vol. 31, No. 1, Winter 1983, pp. 12-20; Hatch, p. 187.

19. Hatch, p. 192.

20. Cited image of Hillary Clinton with tagline, "Condemnation: Leaders including Hillary Clinton and Hamid Karzai have been quick to express their disgust at the Marines' actions as apparently shown in the video," available from *www.dailymail.co.uk/news/article-2085872/Urination-video-4-US-Marines-charged-hours.html.*

21. Cited image of Peter Lavoy, available from *www.cbsnews.com/8301-202_162-57385035/pentagon-official-apologizes-for-koran-burning/.*

22. Cited image of David Cameron, available from *content.time.com/time/specials/packages/article/0,28804,1997272_1997273_1997274,00.html.*

23. Benoit, pp. 1-8; Ware and Linkugel, pp. 274-282.

24. Claudia I. Janssen, "Addressing Corporate Ties to Slavery: Corporate Apologia in a Discourse of Reconciliation," *Communication Studies,* Vol. 63, No. 1, January-March 2012, pp. 18-35.

25. Cited image of William Brandt, available from *content.time.com/time/specials/packages/article/0,28804, 1997272_1997273_1997275,00.html.*

26. William Brandt, as quoted in John Borneman, *Political Crime and the Memory of Loss,* Indianapolis, IN: Indiana University Press, 2011, p. 50.

27. Cited image of Vladmir Putin visiting survivors, available from *www.//upload.wikimedia.org/wikipedia/ commons/2/24/Vladimir_Putin_with_victims_of_Nord-Ost_ terrorism.jpg.*

28. Cited image of George W. and Laura Bush, available from *www.cbsnews.com/news/bush-tours-slaverys-past/.*

29. Cited image of flag raising related to Thomas Pickering's trip to China, available from *www.xtimeline.com/evt/view. aspx?id=144391.*

30. Cited image of Nestor Kirchner, available from *www. crikey.com.au/2010/10/28/letter-from-argentina-and-a-death-that-stopped-the-nation/?wpmp_switcher=mobile.*

31. Cited image of General Allen, available from *www. youtube.com/watch?v=f1zDnmiSG9c.*

32. Cited image of interfaith prayer gathering, available from *calltocompassion.com/media-archive/9-14-01/.*

33. Cited image related to Australian apology, available from *www.safecom.org.au/archives-indigenous.htm.*

34. Janseen, pp. 28-30.

35. *Ibid.,* p. 22, Hatch, p. 191.

36. Cited image related to Rudd's apology to Australian aborigines, available from *www.typingisnotactivism.word-press.com/2008/02/12/full-text-of-australias-apology-to-the-stolen-generations/.*

37. Katharine Q. Seelye, "Clinton Comment on Slavery Draws a Republican Ire," *The New York Times,* March 28, 1998, available from *www.nytimes.com/1998/03/28/us/clinton-comment-on-slavery-draws-a-republican-s-ire.html.*

38. Cited image of William Clinton, available from *www.nola.com/politics/index.ssf/2012/02/saying_im_sorry_is_not_easy_fo.html.*

39. Cited image of Abraham Lincoln, available from *www.richmondmagazine.com/articles/lincoln-in-richmond-10-07-2009.html.*

40. Emil B. Towner: "A <Patriotic> Apologia: The Transcendence of the Dixie Chicks," *Rhetoric Review,* Vol. 29, No. 1, 2010, pp. 293-309.

41. Hatch, p. 208.

42. Cited image of Bishop Tutu and William De Klerk, available from *www.nieman.harvard.edu/reports/article-online-exclusive/100012/manipulator-or-human-rights-facilitator-extended.aspx.*

43. Cited image of Mr. Clinton and Mr. Shaw about the Tuskegee experiments with tagline, "Washington Post photo of survivor Herman Shaw and Bill Clinton," available from *www.sorrywatch.com/2013/04/18/an-apology-for-tuskegee/.*

44. Cited image of Obama's beer summit, available from *www.reuters.com/article/2009/07/31/us-obama-race-idUSTRE56U0KN20090731.*

SECTION II:

PERSPECTIVES ON MESSAGE STRATEGIES
OF ONLINE EXTREMISTS

CHAPTER 4

TEACHING HATE:
THE ROLE OF INTERNET VISUAL IMAGERY IN THE RADICALIZATION OF WHITE ETHNO-TERRORISTS IN THE UNITED STATES

Michael S. Waltman

The Internet has become a powerful tool for white supremacists in the United States seeking to radicalize others to become domestic terrorists. These hate mongers manipulate images and visual aesthetics that promote violence against the "enemies" of white people through powerful appeals to emotions, core beliefs, and identities. White supremacist domestic terrorists construct an ideology of hate that identifies their enemies (e.g., Jews, the Jewish-occupied federal government, African Americans, and illegal immigrants) as worthy of death because they pose a dire threat to white people. They use visual imagery to represent these enemies as animals, diseased, and highly violent. The repeated portrayal of nonwhites through such negative imagery serves as a foundational rationale for violence and domestic terrorism. Therefore, understanding white supremacist domestic terrorism necessitates understanding the process that leads to that terrorism.

This chapter maps the domestic terrorism terrain, describes the visual imagery that potential white domestic terrorists encounter on the Internet, and draws conclusions regarding the process of making domestic terrorists. This chapter argues that the making of domestic terrorists occurs through a three-stage process: the construction of white people as a valued in-group;

the denigration of enemies of white people, including the construction of the enemies as a deadly threat to white people; and the rhetorical conquering of the enemies of white people.

MAPPING THE DOMESTIC TERRORISM TERRAIN

Today, most domestic terrorists are lone wolf ethno-terrorists who, like Oklahoma City bomber Timothy McVeigh, wait for an appropriate time to take violent action on their own against the enemies of the Aryan race.[1] Normally, lone wolves try to avoid public affiliation with specific hate groups in order to protect the entire group and group leaders. Therefore, the number of lone wolves in the United States is unknown, despite the fact that such ethno-terrorism is an all-too-common occurrence. On May 23, 2012, the judicial system convicted and sentenced one such lone wolf, Dennis Mahon, to 40 years in prison for the bombing of the Scottsdale Diversity Director's office, an event that injured the director and his secretary. The U.S. district judge adjudicating this case referred to the bombing as an act of domestic terrorism intended to promote an agenda of hate and racism.[2] In the past, the Internet has played a role in such radicalizations, including recruitment into hate groups, socialization of new members, and the promotion of violence.[3] Sequestered from outside influences, some lone wolf individuals immerse themselves in web material that continually reminds them of the threats to white people. Evidence suggests that killer Benjamin Nathaniel Smith, an ethno-terrorist inspired by Matt Hale (himself convicted of conspiracy to commit murder) and Timothy McVeigh, cocooned himself in cyber hate.[4]

In some cases, however, hate groups and their leaders have inspired lone wolf domestic terrorists. Some of these groups are discussed in the next section. Most explicitly linked to specific hate crimes and ethno-violence are two "race religion" groups: Christian Identity and racist Pre-Christian paganism. White ethno-terrorists have also blended religious beliefs with secular Neo-Nazi and militia beliefs.

Christian Identity Groups.

Christian Identity followers accept a racist version of Christianity that grounds their hatred in a reading of the Christian Bible that portrays Aryans as the "chosen people" of the Old Testament. The Christian Identity god is white, and they believe Jews are the literal spawn of Satan's coitus with Eve in the Garden of Eden. Because they believe Jews (and Satan) are controlling the federal government, Christian Identity adherents are decidedly anti-State.[5] During the 1990s, the Christian Identity Movement insinuated itself into the Militia Movement, only some of whom exhibited hateful inclinations toward Jews and minorities. The Christian Identity Movement members preached that the government wanted to kill white people and that a race war against the government was inevitable. The group provided the Ruby Ridge incident and Waco as evidence for this conspiracy theory. Key figures in the Christian Identity Movement include Louis Beam, Jr., and Richard Butler. Through Butler's church (the Church of Jesus Christ Christian), Beam and Butler radicalized an array of White supremacists (e.g., Klansmen, Neo-Pagans, and racist and anti-government Patriot Groups). They convinced a generation of White supremacists that, in order to bring heaven to

85

earth, they must rid the earth of God's enemies (the government, Jews, and other nonwhite people). Many who heard this message believed them. Through writings such as *Why We Have to Kill the Bastards, Seditious Conspiracy*, and *Leaderless Resistance*, Beam urged the American Hate Movement to make explicit shifts toward paramilitarization and violence.[5]

A number of domestic terrorists subscribing to the Christian Identity Church have played an important role in the anti-abortion movement. Christian Identity adherents see abortions as an obstacle to supplying white soldiers for this impending "race war." Such thinking made both white women who receive abortions and abortionists a threat to the white race. Several reasonably well-known instances of White ethno-terrorist killings have ties to the Identity Church Movement. Verne Jay Merrell, Charles Barbee, and Robert Berry, for example, robbed a local bank to finance their violence and bombed both Planned Parenthood and the *Spokesman Review* newspaper in Spokane Washington. All three claimed to be members of the Phineas Priesthood sect. The Phineas Priesthood is a subgroup of the Christian Identity Movement. Members claim membership by killing a member of an interracial couple. Another highly publicized instance occurred in 2003 when authorities arrested Eric Rudolph after he had eluded law enforcement for over 5 years. Ultimately, law enforcement officials charged and convicted Rudolph of four terrorist bombings between 1996 and 1998. His targets included an abortion clinic, a gay bar, and the 1996 Olympic games (the latter because it celebrated globalism and multiculturalism). Rudolph's nail bombs were particularly effective at wounding and crippling his targets.[6]

Pre-Christian Paganism.

Racist Pre-Christian paganism sprang from the belief that Christianity is fundamentally a Jewish religion, a religion of the weak (since Jesus, a Jew, preached forgiveness and tolerance of those who are different), and a religion insufficiently radical to mobilize actions against the enemies of white people. Pre-Christian pagans draw on the values of the Anglo-Saxon warrior culture and celebrate the good death. The good death was one obtained in the heat of battle and in defense of king and kinsmen. Stories of such deaths passed from one generation to the next. The original pagans practiced human sacrifice and ritual killings of their captured enemies. Today's generation of racist Pre-Christian pagans view ethno-violence as a form of human sacrifice made to Thor or Odin. They develop Blots (prayer rituals) performed prior to an ethnic killing in order to bring Odin's good graces to the murder(s). In this sense, violence emerges from the very fabric of racist Pre-Christian paganism.

Robert Matthews, venerated as a martyr of the American Hate Movement, is an important icon among racist Pre-Christian pagans. Matthews organized a group called the Order. He recruited a small group of Klansmen, Neo-Nazis, and Christian Identity adherents whose purpose was to provoke the inevitable race war that must consume America. Matthews used his racist pagan religious beliefs and rituals to imbue the group with a common worldview. The Order robbed a Brinks armored car of $3.6 million to finance their racial holy war. The Order captured the imagination of the public at large when members killed Denver "shock radio jock" Allen Greensburg for insulting them when they called into his radio show. Eventually, Robert Matthews would die "the good death" in a gun battle with Federal Bureau of Investigation (FBI) agents. Today, racists of all stripes memorialize Matthews on the Internet. The judicial system convicted members of the Order of murder and armed robbery. One of the members, the late David Lane, would become the intellectual and spiritual leader of modern-day racist Odinism, the fastest growing and most violent of race religions.

While the Order serves as an exemplar of the ethno-violence weaved into the fabric of Neo-paganism, other examples illustrate the violence perpetuated in the name of this race religion. In June 1998, John King murdered James Byrd by dragging him to death in Jasper, Texas. King became a Neo-pagan while in jail for prior crimes. He hoped to gain notoriety in the dragging of Byrd that he could subsequently use to start his own hate group. King and two other accomplices left Byrd's decapitated body on the lawn of an African American church to ensure full understanding of their message. Another example of a racist pagan was Leo Felton, who authorities arrested before his group, Aryan Unit One, could carry out their plans to bomb Boston's Holocaust Museum and other targets. On August 10, 1999, Aryan Nations' member Buford Furrow walked into a Los Angeles Jewish community center and began to shoot, leaving a 69-year-old receptionist and four children wounded and traumatized. His purpose was to awaken white people to what he perceived was a Jewish international conspiracy committed to the oppression of white people, and to take some measure of revenge for the FBI's killing of Robert Matthews.[7]

Militia/Patriot Groups.

The extremely violent militia movement of the 1990s is the final exemplar of domestic terrorism and ethno-violence discussed here. Not all militia groups are racist, but many are, due, in part to the Christian Identity infiltration of the militia/patriot groups. These often anti-Semitic groups view the federal government under the control of Jewish interests. Militia groups tend to organize around a fevered commitment to the second amendment. They see the accumulation of firearms, eternal vigilance to the threat of the government, and ongoing training and military exercises as the only way to keep the federal government in check.

Perhaps it seems a little odd that a group of working and middle-class Americans are keeping the Zionist Occupied Government (ZOG) in check by going out into the wilderness of Michigan or Ohio to train for battle against the federal government. But this is only an oddity if one does not view the world through the militia's ideological lens. Militia members view their current behavior and beliefs as profoundly American, consonant with the myth that militias have played an important role in American history. They view themselves as the modern embodiment of the character Mel Gibson portrays in *The Patriot*.[8]

Timothy McVeigh, with his militia beliefs and connections to the Identity Church movement, followed instructions for building a truck bomb he found in the racist novel, *The Turner Diaries*. Until the attacks of September 11, 2001, this bombing was the most deadly act of domestic terrorism in U.S. history, killing 168 men, women, and children and wounding another 895. Highly visible (but failed prosecutions) against militia personnel contribute to the anti-government hatred of militia groups. The government's failure to convict Louis Beam with sedition in Arkansas in 1987 added credence to the militia narrative that the government was willing to persecute innocent citizens on false charges.[9] Recently, authorities charged the Huttaree militia in Michigan, a Christian militia preparing to fight an end-of-times battle with Satan and his earthly representatives, with plotting to kill Michigan law enforcement officers.[10] When the courts dismissed the case against the Huttaree in April 2012, the federal government again appeared to militia members as a sinister force persecuting American citizens.[11]

Presently, the number of anti-government militia/patriot groups is at an all-time high. The Southern Poverty Law Center's Intelligence Report notes that the number of groups rose from 824 in 2010 to 1,274 last year, well over the record high during the first wave of militia groups in the 1990s.[12] Between 1990 and 2010, these "far rightest" groups had involvement in 345 homicide incidents and killed almost 50 law enforcement officers. Today's militia rhetoric is as apocalyptic as the rhetoric of the 1990s. In Pensacola, Florida, a militia leader and retired FBI agent tells militia members, "The federal government has set up 1,000 internment camps across the country and is storing 30,000 guillotines and a half-million caskets in Atlanta."[13] In Lexington, Massachusetts, a leader of the militia group Oath Keepers tells followers: "We're in perilous times . . . perhaps more perilous than in 1775."[14]

Recently, racist militia groups have reached out to Nativist groups such as the Minutemen who have long patrolled the Mexican-United States border in order to prevent the "Mexican invasion" of the United States by illegal immigrants. Increasingly, militia group rhetoric is taking on a more Nativist tone.[15] In part, the explanation for the merger of the two types of extremist groups stems from the violence and killing of illegal immigrants that have sent Minutemen to prison for murder or that have resulted in the death of Minutemen themselves.[16]

VISUAL IMAGERY ON THE INTERNET AND RADICALIZATION

The balance of this chapter examines the ways that various hate websites manipulate visual imagery to radicalize white ethno-terrorists in the United States. This chapter explores the use of hate discourse and images on webpages maintained by a range of hate groups and hate mongers for the last 10 years. This research examines how hate visual imagery (i.e., cartoons, comics, on-line games, and artwork) helps radicalize by: (a) recruiting new members, (b) socializing recruited members, (c) cultivating a collective form of memory that encourages identification with the group, and (d) promoting ethno-violence.[17] This examination of cartoons, artwork, and visual imagery focuses primarily on materials from the *Vanguard News Network* (VNN), *White Aryan Resistance* (WAR), *The Insurgent, Tightrope,* and the *Jim Crow Museum of Racist Memorabilia.*[18]

VALUING THE IN-GROUP

Viewers of various hate websites learn to view Aryans as builders of high culture superior to all other races. Many cartoons portray white people as a valuable and cohesive in-group. One recurrent theme is that white people are builders of civilization. The art available on *The Insurgent* is reminiscent of posters one might find on a young white supremacist's bedroom wall. One such poster presents the image of a strong, good-looking white man wearing a hardhat and work shirt. In the background is the skyline of a city, a bridge resembling the Golden Gate Bridge, and an airplane in ascent. At the top of the poster are the words, "White Men Built this Nation," and at the bottom of the poster, "White Men *are* this Nation!!" Such a poster proffers that not only are white men responsible for building our society, but the appropriate American identity is a white identity.[19]

A recent cartoon in VNN portrays white people as the builders of western civilization. In the frame's background, a painter, a musician, and a writer create three of the great products of western civilization. In the foreground, a Satanic figure of a Jew whispers into the ear of an attractive blond woman, "Yes, my dear . . . White men love to oppress and destroy. They are cruel disgusting rapists with no sense of humanity." This cartoon celebrates the superiority of the white race, while simultaneously reminding readers of the threat Jews pose to racial purity.

Several posters portray Aryans as the inheritors of a grand and glorious pagan Viking tradition. The initiated "reader" of these posters will understand that they connect the reader to this glorious Aryan past and make one a part of a community superior to all others.[20] One poster, for example, depicts a Viking warrior leaning against the bow of a Viking ship. Celtic knots border the top of the poster. At the foot of the Viking ship is a representation of Mjolnir, Thor's hammer, long understood as a symbol of power to pagans. Above the Viking's head is the message: "As

92

Our Ancestors Before Us, Our Kinsmen Must Always be Prepared to Fight—For There is Nothing More Horrible than Cultural or National Obliteration." The cartoonist draws each "t" as an upward pointing arrow. The upward pointing arrow, the Tyre rune, is the racist pagan symbol for warfare and battle. Thus, the initiated reader views vigilance as coterminous with war and violence.

Another example of this glorified in-group occurs in a poster with two shirtless Aryan men. The man in the background is a Viking specter holding a battle-ax in his left hand. The man in the foreground is a modern man wearing a Mjolnir pendant. Throughout the poster, racist pagan symbols appear in highly visible ways. Above and beside the men is the message:

> If one day we can visualize and create a new yet very old white awareness who, conscious of soul, race, and history, unhesitatingly proclaims the old yet new values, then around this nucleus will gather all who stumble in darkness though rooted in ancient soil of our European homeland.

Here again, the image of the white man as builder of society appears in these "superior" Aryan bloodlines.

THE OUT-GROUP

Denigration.

In sharp contrast to the portrayal of the in-group members, white supremacists strongly denigrate those outside of the Aryan race. Numerous cartoons depict Mexicans as dirty, unkempt, lacking in personal responsibility, and a drag on society. One cartoon presents one such Mexican as holding an outline of the

United States labeled "United States of Mexico." The artist poses the question: "Hey, White man. Where will you go when *this* happens?" The artist draws on a reality that many white people fear, specifically, that within a generation, white people will be in the minority in the United States.[21] Other cartoons allude to the large number of illegal immigrants coming into the United States as an attempt to "re-take" the southwestern United States for Mexico. When cartoons represent Mexican women, the females are almost always shown pregnant. Such images depict Mexicans as a drain on public resources and as taking American jobs from Americans and retaking America by out-breeding whites. One cartoon presents a drawing of a naked, pregnant Mexican woman with the message, ". . . How do Mexicans reproduce so rapidly? Research has revealed their female offspring are actually born pregnant!"[22] The websites recurrently present Mexican fecundity as a threat to the white race and "traditional" white control of America and American resources.

Similarly, white supremacist websites visually portray African Americans as black predators. A cartoon from VNN explicitly portrays this threat. A menacing black youth robs a middle-aged couple in an alley. A newspaper pictured on the ground includes a headline that reads, "Rise in Crime." With their hands in the air, the husband of the couple remarks, "Oh thank God, You're a 'N-word'!!! For a second, we thought you were a terrorist."[23]

The threat posed by the "other" to white America includes character portrayals of Jews as corrupters of white women. One way the websites portray the risk to white women is their focus on the Jews' supposed penchant for encouraging the mixing of the races. According to the online sites, Jews, guilty of conspiring to wage genocide against the white race, control mainstream Hollywood and television programming and use that control to depict interracial relationships. For example, a cartoon from VNN entitled "Herschel Danglestein Directs" suggests that Jewish youth learn such an approach at an early age. Herschel begins by telling the reader that his teacher, Mr. Silverstein, asked him to direct his school's production of "Romeo and Juliet." Herschel tells the reader that while Jenny Smith (represented in his thoughts as a blond white girl) agreed to play Juliet, he does not know whom to cast as Romeo. In the next panel, an African American youth walks by Herschel and his teacher. The mischievous Herschel smiles and calls after the young man, "Oh, Leroy. . . ." In short, the strip constructs Jews as a genocidal threat to the white race by encouraging a mixing of the races.

The strip also depicts Herschel as a genocidal threat in a series of cartoons when he takes a job as an advice columnist in his Uncle Shlomo's newspaper. It illustrates that Jews control the media and use it to threaten the purity of the white race. In these cartoons, Herschel encourages a white woman to choose her black boyfriend over her family and encourages a white wife and mother to leave her family to satisfy her own emotional needs. In a cartoon entitled "Television is the Deadliest Drug of All . . . and the Jews are its Pushers," a Jewish face on a television screen is overseeing the injection of a white woman with a needle. Words printed on the syringe read, "Having sex with the Negro will make you popular." These cartoons vilify the Jewish and African American identities, while warning the white man of the out-group's intentions. This same theme appears in more recent cartoons from VNN. One image, in particular, is most poignant: A white man is sitting in front of a large-screen HD television as a hand holding an automatic handgun extends from the television, shooting the viewer through the head.

Various cartoons also portray the federal government as controlled by Zionist interests, the ZOG and the Jewish International Conspiracy. In a cartoon entitled "A Traditional Jewish Pastime," Little Herschel Danglestein is playing with his puppet, manipulating the puppet's strings and making it dance. The cartoonist places George Bush's head on the puppet's body, and he is holding an Israeli flag while shouting, "Let's roll!" Here, the cartoonist is making an obvious allusion to the claim that Israel manipulated the response to the attacks of 9/11.

The most recent VNN cartoons also portray the ZOG conspiracy. The author of the cartoon uses the 2008 presidential election to show the farce of the American political elections. Cartoon images of both "Juan McCain and Obamanation" appear. Banners behind McCain emphasize his support for Mexican immigrants (including an oversized sombrero and illegal immigrants wearing t-shirts that support La Raza) and "100 more years of support for Israel." Below Juan McCain's name is the slogan "Captain Amnesty" and "Jew Puppet." Below Obamanation, we see "Mongrel Fool and Jewish Tool." Obama appears satisfied as a young blond woman performs oral sex on him. Surrounding his image are supporters waving signs in support of hate speech laws, continuation of affirmative action, more welfare, and "you ease my white guilt." The message is clear: Israel controls both Republicans and Democrats and will use the government to hurt white people.

In sum, domestic extremists employ a host of cartoons and other visual imagery to portray Mexicans, African Americans, and Jews as imminent threats to White America. A set of cartoons and visual imagery discussed in the next section offers the solution to such threats, as rhetorical conquest emerges as the necessary way to manage the vile threat the out-groups pose to white America.

Rhetorically Conquer the Out-Group.

Online games allow the hate monger to conquer the out-group rhetorically. Many online games position the player to take the point of view of a shooter or bomber and accumulate points by killing members of the out-group.[24] The game, *Watch Out Behind You, Hunter*, allows the game player to conquer gay men symbolically by hunting and killing gay rapists. Another game, *Border Patrol,* allows the player to "hunt" Mexicans "jumping" the border. As Mexicans run across the computer screen, the player is able to score points by shooting the "border jumpers" who explode with blood and screams when shot. A game entitled *Bin Laden Liquors* allows players to shoot the image of Bin Laden who peeks from behind a counter of a ransacked liquor store.

A new game on *The Insurgent* is entitled *Kaboom: The Suicide Bombing Game*. In the game, a suicide bomber skulks through the streets of a typical American city as other pedestrians pass by. The goal is to blow one's self up while killing as many citizens as possible. Victims scream while exploding in a soup of blood and bones. Immediately thereafter, a score appears on the computer screen listing the number of men, women, and children killed. Arguably, when players repeat these games time after time, they may eventually come to see themselves killing their enemies in real life.[25] Notably, Islamist terrorist groups use comparable "first person shooter" games to the same end.

Cartoons of domestic terrorist websites also depict the pleasure of murder. A cartoon found in *The Insurgent* advocates the murder of illegal Mexican immigrants. A group of Mexicans look on in horror when they encounter the decapitated head of a "border jumper" on a spike. The caption reads: "Hey America, want to know a way to stop the flow of illegal immigrants from Mexico?"[26] This theme plays out time and again in online cartoons. A few examples include the depiction of a racist Neo-pagan bashing in the skull of an African American, a Ku Klux Klan bride and groom driving away from their wedding and dragging African Americans behind their car, and a Klansman shooting an African American in the face to prevent him from dating the Klansman's daughter.

A number of cartoons portray the pleasure of murder through references to a Racial Holy War (RAHOWA). One cartoon from the *Jim Crow Museum of Racist Memorabilia* presents a white man on his knees. His hair is in dreadlocks and he wears a t-shirt printed with the words, "Rasta Rules." In the background is a blond, white woman holding an African American toddler. She, too, has a gun pointed at her head. The caption reads, "Attention all Whiggers and Mixers . . . After the Day of Reckoning race traitors will be the first to go." A recent VNN cartoon incorporates the same theme. Ann Dunham, President Obama's white mother, appears in hell where flames consume her and "Mudsharks" participate in the eternal tearing and ripping of her skin. From the perspective of VNN readers, the "contamination" of the white gene pool by a Kenyan justifies the punishment of Obama's mother. The cartoon celebrates the death of a race-traitor and takes pleasure in the imagined suffering of a soul. The cartoon is not unlike an image that appeared on the webpage of the Westboro Baptist Church showing an image of Matthew Shepherd, a young man murdered in Laramie because he was gay. A clicker below Matthew's image kept track of the number of days he had been in hell.

Online graphic comics portray handsome and heroic Aryan figures wreaking their righteous vengeance on evil Jews and African Americans. Through shotgun blasts, staccato automatic weapons fire, beheadings with axes, and a mass poisoning with ricin, we see strong Aryans calmly finding pleasure, peace, and serenity through ethno-violence.[27]

CONCLUSION

Strategically, cyber hate offers a plethora of images that appear specifically designed to cultivate a violent orientation to the challenges facing white people. First, white readers learn that they are descendants of a racially-superior group who brought the world everything that is good: western civilization, science, high-forms of art and culture, medicine, and an economics that gives people the leisure time to create. Second, white people learn that inferior Jews and "mud" races want to destroy white people. For many, the election of America's first African American President serves as evidence that white people have lost America. Third, and most importantly, readers learn that violence is a reasonable response with an outcome of ultimate success against this threat. This research illustrates the way that visual images attempt to radicalize white people to hate and attack their host of enemies. The Internet is quite unique in its ability to use vivid and compelling imagery to radicalize potential white domestic terrorists. Internet imagery makes an enemy more disgusting, dangerous, and deserving of death than other communication tools.

ENDNOTES - CHAPTER 4

1. Lane Crothers, *Rage on the Right: The American Militia Movement from Ruby Ridge to Homeland Security*, New York: Rowman & Littlefield Publishers, 2003.

2. Jacques Billeaud, "Dennis Mahon Sentencing: White Supremacist Faces Prison Time After Package Bomb Attack," *Huffington Post*, 2012, available from *www.huffingtonpost.com/2012/05/22/dennis-mahon-setenced-don-logan_n_1537003.html*.

3. Michael S. Waltman and John H. Haas, *The Communication of Hate*, New York: Peter Lang Publishing, 2011; Crothers; William Guttentag and Vince DiPersio, "Hate.com: Extremists on the Internet," J. Anderson, prod., *America Undercover*, Home Box Office, 2003.

4. Guttentag and DiPersio.

5. Aaron Winter, "Beam, Louis, Jr. (1946-)," Jeffery Ian Ross, ed., *Encyclopedia of Religion and Violence: An Encyclopedia of Faith and Conflict from Antiquity to the Present*, Armonk, NY: M. E. Sharpe, Inc., 2011, p. 101.

6. The Reverend W. N. Ortwell also claimed to be a Phineas Priest when he participated in armed standoffs with federal agents in 1996 and 1997 in Texas. Willie Ray Lamply served time in prison for plotting to blow up abortion clinics, gay bars, Anti-Defamation League offices, and the Southern Poverty Law Center. Paul Hill shot and killed Dr. John Britton after receiving information about Britton's schedule and home address from anti-abortion protestors. In 2003, James Kopp pled guilty to shooting Dr. Barnett Slepian through his kitchen window in 1998. Kopp

was also suspected in four other shootings of abortion doctors in New York and Canada. See Michael Waltman, "Christian Identity Movement," Ross, ed., p. 147.

7. Michael Waltman, "Pre-Christian Paganism," in Ross, ed., p. 585.

8. Crothers, p. 30. Perhaps one of the reasons that this militia myth remains a significant part of our collective American memory is because those founding fathers supporting a strong federal government used the militia myth to comfort those who feared a strong federal government. American militias, they argued, will again come to the aid of her citizens should a strong federal government ever behave like the English monarchy.

9. Winter, p. 101.

10. "Christian Warrior Militia Accused in Plot to Kill Police," CNN, March 30, 2010, available from *www.cnn.com/2010/CRIME/03/29/michigan.arrests/index.html*.

11. Matthew Dolan, "Charges Dismissed in Michigan Militia Case," *The Wall Street Journal*.

12. Mark Potok, "Georgia on our Mind," *Intelligence Report*, Montgomery, AL: Southern Poverty Law Center, (SPLC), 2012, available from *www.splcenter.org/get-informed/intelligence-report/browse-all-issues/2012/spring*.

13. Larry Keller, "The Second Wave: Evidence Grows of Far-right Militia Resurgence," *Intelligence Report*, 135, SPLC, Fall 2009, available from *www.splcenter.org/get-informed/intelligence-report/browse-all-issues/2009/fall/the-second-wave*.

14. *Ibid.*

15. According to Keller, "In fact, the anti-immigration movement is both fueling and helping to racialize the anti-government Patriot resurgence. More and more, members of the Nativist groups like the Minutemen are adopting core militia ideas and fears." Thus, Minutemen groups are beginning to see illegal immigration as a symptom of a broader problem. As one Minuteman

put it: "We're still concerned about the border intruders, but since this all started we've become aware of the fact that border intruders are *just pawns in the big game*." See David Holthouse, "Nativists to patriots: Nativist vigilantes adopt 'patriot,'" Intelligence Report, SPLC, available from *www.splcenter.org/get-informed/ intelligence-report/browse-all-issues/2009/fall/nativists-to-patriots.*

16. Heidi Beirich, "The Year Nativism," *Intelligence Report,* SPLC, 2012, available from *www.splcenter.org/get-informed/intelligence-report/browse-all-issues/2012/spring.* The threat of militia violence is ongoing. Recently, four members of the North Georgia Militia (Frederick Thomas, Emory Dan Roberts, Samuel Crump, Jr., and Ray Adams) were arrested based on hundreds of hours of conversations between the men, secretly recorded by informants. Tapes provide evidence of the men discussing the possible assassination of Attorney General, Eric Holder, and numerous government operatives—"IRS [Internal Revenue Service], ATF [Alcohol, Tobacco, and Firearms], FBI [Federal Bureau of Investigation], and cops." See Bill Morlin, "Militia Madness," *Intelligence Report,* SPLC, 2012, available from *www.splcenter.org/get-informed/intelligence-report/browse-all-issues/2012/spring.* The men, aged from 65 to 73, and family members used their age as evidence that these were simply old, nearly senile men engaged in harmless, venting banter. Age did not, however, prevent 88-year-old Neo-Nazi James von Brunn from murdering a security guard at the U.S. Holocaust Museum, Washington, DC, before being killed himself. See Leah Nelson, "The Wife's Tale: Married to a Neo-Nazi," *Intelligence Report,* SPLC, 2012, available from *www.splcenter.org/ get-informed/intelligence-report/browse-all-issues/2012/spring.*

17. Waltman and Haas, pp. 63-83.

18. Vanguard News Network, available from *www.vanguardnewsnetwork.com/cartoonsgraphics/* and *www.vanguardnewsnetwork. com/v1/; Insurgent,* available from *www.resist.com/racistgames/index.htm; Tightrope,* available from *www.tightrope.cc/kotc/comic.htm; Jim Crow Museum of Racist Memorabilia,* available from *www.ferris. edu/jimcrow/cartoons/.*

19. Waltman and Haas, p. 74.

20. Mattias Gardell, *Gods of the Blood: The Pagan Revival and White Separatism*, Durham, NC, and London, UK: Duke University Press, 2003, p. 1.

21. Sam Roberts, "In a Generation, Minorities May be the U.S. Majority," *The New York Times*, 2008, available from *www.nytimes.com/2008/08/14/washington/14census.html?_r=3&th&emc=th&oref=slogin*.

22. See *www.resist.com/CARTOON%20GALLERY/SPICS/spics_image03.jpg*.

23. See *www.vanguardnewsnetwork.com/v1/cartoons18.htm*.

24. Waltman and Haas, p. 77.

25. *Ibid.*, p. 81.

26. *Ibid.*, pp. 79-80.

27. *Ibid.*, pp. 64-84.

CHAPTER 5

"COUNTER" OR "ALTERNATIVE": CONTESTING VIDEO NARRATIVES OF VIOLENT ISLAMIST EXTREMISM

Scott W. Ruston
Jeffry R. Halverson

Testifying before the Senate Foreign Relations Committee in 2011, Secretary of State Hillary Rodham Clinton declared that the United States was losing the information war in its struggle against al-Qaeda and affiliated movements (AQAM).[1] The fact that she characterized the situation in militaristic terms is consistent with the prevailing U.S. approach to strategic communication: increase funding for the "big guns" of state broadcasting (e.g., Voice of America) and get "our message into places."[2] This approach belies the lingering presence of an outdated message-influence model of communication. In this model, the right message inserted at the right place will have the desired effect. Interceding with an opposing message requires disrupting the transmission method or disarming the content.

In recent years, online videos produced by AQAM and their supporters have become part of the "information war" that Secretary Clinton described, and have thus garnered the attention of the military, security professionals, and academics.[3] The videos AQAM produces have had an impact on several international conflicts, and studies of these information campaigns have focused primarily on the propaganda effects of these videos and their recruitment impact. However, insufficient attention has been directed toward online videos as part of a cultural narrative landscape. More than campaigns designed to affect perception of specific events, the entry of AQAM videos into the global online environment represents an alarming spread of its ideology. The spread and recirculation of these videos among noncombatants is a growing concern, as the struggle against AQAM increasingly moves from battlefield confrontation to a political and ideological contest, whereby AQAM earns the right to govern a community not through fear of attack, but through garnering the consent of the citizenry.

The disarming of AQAM propaganda messages is the domain of the U.S. Department of State's Center for Strategic Counterterrorism Communication (CSCC). Charged with "countering the actions and ideologies of al-Qaeda, its affiliates and adherents, other terrorism organizations and violent extremists overseas," the CSCC and its Digital Outreach Team (DOT) corrects misinformation, engages in open dialogue, and focuses "on narratives that can positively influence those who may be susceptible to radicalization and recruitment by terrorist organizations."[4] The CSCC's mandate to engage in dialogue with audiences targeted by AQAM propaganda is a major step forward, moving away from the message-influence model and embracing a more complex, dialogue-driven perspective on communication.[5] Nevertheless, those who implement the CSCC directive do so as *counter-narrative*.

As Christian Leuprecht *et al.* have argued, the counter-narrative approach has certain flaws.[6] The emphasis on a singular, antidote narrative falls victim to the same ineffectuality and lack of suitability as the message-influence model. Human communication is far more complex, and approaches to persuasion, outreach, and messaging must recognize the involvement of multiple audiences. By providing close analysis of the visual narrative features of AQAM and supporter videos, this chapter proposes a means of operationalizing Leuprecht's call for recognition of multiple voices and grievances.

In order to clarify the importance of these videos, we establish the link between these videos and the transition from terrorists using media as a means to exercise coercion (motivating through violence and fear) to their use of media for consent building. Next, we analyze the phenomenon and explore prominent narrative elements that require attention and awareness in order to pursue an effective means of narrative-based engagement. The narrative elements we discuss include not only form and content, but also the broader socio-cultural communication environment in which these videos circulate. In doing so, we also address existing efforts by the U.S. Government designed to counter extremist messaging through online videos. In our view, these efforts are important and notable but would greatly benefit from a more systematic approach informed by narrative analysis. In the process, we propose a narrative-based strategy to craft a new generation of strategic communication using online videos, shifting greater attention from counter-narrative to *alternative* narrative.

MEDIA AND POLITICAL COERCION

Modern terrorism has always had a symbiotic relationship with the media, as terrorists depend on mass media to spread news of an attack widely and amplify the fear that results.[7] The emergence of accessible online videos has become a new front in the "war for hearts and minds," as these videos have shifted from solely depicting or claiming credit for a terrorist act to a broader media campaign with a wide range of content, styles, producers, and audiences. These videos exhibit an ideologically grounded pursuit of communicative and persuasive acts, operating within the domain of civil society, designed to garner the support and consent of a contested population.[8] Professionally produced videos by the official media divisions of established organizations (e.g., al-Qaeda's As-Sahab) certainly operate in this domain. Perhaps more disconcerting, though, is the rise of amateur, pro-AQAM video content. These videos take a variety of forms and have steadily increased in sophistication as advances in affordable technology have made video production easier than ever before. They also exhibit characteristics common to global remix culture.

The contested populations that both AQAM media divisions and sympathetic amateurs target are not deeply committed to either the extremist cause and ideology, or to the government and agents of the status quo. Video producers could potentially sway them either way. The "war of ideas" and "the battle for hearts and minds" are popular phrases for the range of efforts designed to garner the consent of these populations. Dr. Cori E. Dauber's study (and others, see, e.g., Jarret Brachman) concludes that campaigns for influence are not solely about coercion by force.[9] The West has long viewed terrorism through this lens—as a force to be countered with greater force—considering terrorist groups as elements of political society. However, these cases suggest that coercion plays an increasingly secondary role to the campaigns designed to seek consent; thus, AQAM can be seen as an element of civil society (appropriate given their heavy emphasis on instruction, religious interpretation, even local civic governance), which exercises power and control through consent. Notably, the extremists do not need full-blown support. They need not gain entire ideologically committed populations. Rather, they simply need to foster acceptance, tolerance, and an aversion to other options. To many, these hegemonic processes are as equally problematic as the coercive tactics of suicide bombings, improvised explosive devices (IEDs) and other violent acts.[10]

To explore fully the challenge the U.S. Government faces, this analysis examines the videos produced by official AQAM media divisions, such as As-Sahab, and the increasingly common prosumer mashups created by sympathetic pro-AQAM amateurs.[11] The AQAM videos exhibit a high degree of professionalism in their production value. They have developed a wider range of content from the days of smuggled audiocassettes. Today's media products emanating from As-Sahab and similar groups frequently carry the appearance of news journalism: a host explains conditions and introduces clips (often of battle scenes). Thus, the AQAM videos are particularly important because they enter into the communication environment purporting to be news. Furthermore, they provide direct access for audience members to the exhortations of the chief ideologues of AQAM.

Amateur, or "jihobbyist," produced videos are equally important and increasingly more difficult to distinguish from AQAM-produced content. Brachman coined the term "jihobbyist" in *Global Jihadism*. It refers to enthusiasts or fans of al-Qaeda's global jihadist movement (which seeks to achieve Muslim autonomy and Islamist governance through violent revolutionary means) that fervently enjoy watching and supporting their agenda and actions, but have no formal connection to AQAM.[12] These jihobbyists are important because they further distribute the AQAM message, build sites, "fan" archives, and infiltrate and incorporate popular culture. Their videos also reveal what jihobbyists as outsider "fans" of AQAM admire most about the jihadist agenda. For instance, while an As-Sahab video may feature one of Ayman al-Zawahiri's long speeches, a jihobbyist video will feature the highlights, stolen footage from Hollywood films (e.g., *Kingdom of Heaven*) and the latest popular *nasheed* (devotional song). The differences in the two types of videos offer analysts important insights into the appeal of AQAM message campaigns.

Finally, the sources of video production also share increasing similarities. This blurring between AQAM productions, mainstream traditional media, and jihobbyist videos reveals the open and fluid nature of the Internet domain. The proliferation of excerpts from official AQAM videos appearing in jihobbyist content suggests shifting power structures. Brachman has argued that Zawahiri's approach, deeply rooted in the lecture format, encourages audiences to take up military jihad against the West; however, Abu Musab al-Suri has long been an advocate for a distributed media jihad.[13] As isolation and drone strikes increasingly marginalize AQAM leaders, al-Suri's approach aligns with a media campaign to build consent. Notably, recent videos, such as *"As Sahab Media Lions of Jihad Part 1,"*[14] exhibit stylistic traits of popular culture. In this example, 3D fly-through animations reminiscent of video games depict extremist heroes and sculptural renditions of the *shahada* (the Islamic creed) throughout the video.[15]

NARRATIVE LANDSCAPES

Understanding the narrative implication of terrorist propaganda videos requires a more sophisticated understanding of "narrative" than the simplistic use of the term as a synonym for "story." A story is a sequence of related events that includes a (sometimes implied) resolution. The following sequence of events is a story: The U.S. infidel soldiers' convoy crossed the highway in Sarwahzah, and the mujahideen sprang their trap. The IED destroyed two tanks and killed nine Americans.[16] A narrative is a system of interrelated stories.[17] Numerous similar stories abound on extremist websites, sometimes with different attackers, victims, and events. Together, these interrelated stories constitute a narrative of mujahideen as the champions able to defeat the invading Western Crusaders. By understanding narrative as a system, we can better understand how narratives can operate at multiple levels.[18] A narrative is a socio-cultural entity, and it serves a cognitive process of understanding and attention. Narratives (whether specific objects like videos, films, or books) operate as systems, both macro- and micro-, comprised of components such as stories, story forms, tropes, archetypes, and so forth. Thus, a socio-cultural object such as an online video might represent a self-contained, small narrative. Or an online video might contain various story elements that work together in a broader macro-narrative system comprised of stories and micro-narratives found in multiple videos, blog posts, speeches, and other sources.

To illustrate this idea further, take an online mash-up video that juxtaposes pictures of Muslims suffering at the hands of U.S. soldiers (e.g., Abu Ghraib) with found-footage of American cruise missiles launching from ships. This content is operating in a larger narrative system that positions the entire Muslim community (*ummah*) as victims of U.S. aggression. Extremists advance this narrative by positioning themselves as archetypal champions and martyrs who will defend and deliver the *ummah* from this suffering and injustice. This is frequently done through videos that celebrate suicide bombers, valorize slain fighters, or extol attacks, such as the jihobbyist video, "*Al-Jihad fisabilil-lah.*"[19] Thus, multiple, unrelated videos that circulate in the common arena of the Internet collectively produce meaning. These narratives are selective in their arrangement of material, and they operate to shape opinion as perceptions. As John Lucaites and Celeste Condit observe, narratives "thus provide an understanding for how the material reality holds together and functions" as well as incorporate "ideal cultural values . . . that constitute a community" and, in so doing, act as vehicles of ideology.[20]

This vast array of cultural expression that circulates in a community or region is what we call the *narrative landscape.*[21] The geographic metaphor is apt, because a landscape includes specific features, such as trees, hills, and rivers, and these features all interact in an ecological system. Yet, landscapes and their systems have characteristics (rugged, serene, etc.) that influence how humans understand a locale and how they interact with it. The same is true with narrative landscapes: stories, narrative systems, and other forms of communication that enter into the narrative landscape interact with those already present. Literary theorist Mikhail Bakhtin describes this interactive quality when he explains:

> Each utterance [story, narrative, communication, etc.] refutes, affirms, supplements, and relies upon the others, presupposes them to be known, and somehow takes them into account.[22]

Demonstrating the applicability of these qualities in political and strategic communication contexts, Tamar Katriel and Aliza Shenhar have applied Bakhtin's theory to the contested discourse surrounding Israeli settlement policy,[23] and our approach extends this application to the environment of online pro-AQAM videos. The narrative landscape is an extremely dynamic and confusing place, but as Lance Bennett and Murray Edelman point out in their analysis of political news stories and narrative processes:

> people notice or ignore news stories according to whether they fit their concerns or aspirations, typically focusing on those that have meaning for them regardless of their compatibility with other narratives.[24]

Within the narrative landscape, visual elements play particularly important roles. The narrative landscape of American politics in 2010-12 witnessed the visual invocation of the Boston Tea Party narrative through political activists dressed in 18th-century colonialist costumes. When flashed on television during a news report, or posted online in a partisan blog, visual images of 21st-century citizens marching in period dress connected the contemporary actions with the broader tax revolt narrative. More frequently, images serve as symbols representing a cultural value common in the narrative landscape. The image of a lion, for example, is a frequent visual symbol of fierceness in battle among jihadist videos. Simple videos such as

"Song for Islam in Complete Competition Version"[25] show an image of a lion while Arabic devotional songs are sung. Others like *"I Cry A Lot to this Song (Nasheed)"*[26] intercut the images of lions with battle images (destroyed buildings, dead bodies, etc.), suggesting those perpetrating the acts are the Lions of Islam.[27]

Understanding AQAM videos in the context of narrative is important for two main reasons. First, ongoing conflicts powerfully illustrate that combat operations alone cannot successfully confront AQAM alone. The battle has shifted from protecting civilians from violence to a much more complex environment, where consent must be nurtured and managed. The struggle to earn the consent of the masses depends on the circulation of ideologies, and as the *U.S. Army/Marine Corps Counterinsurgency Field Manual* points out, "Insurgent groups like al-Qaeda use narratives very effectively in developing legitimating ideologies."[28] Thus, narrative is a vehicle for ideology[29] and participates in the "logic of good reasons" as articulated by communication theorist Walter Fisher.[30]

Fisher's conception of the narrative paradigm, which suggests that humans make sense of the world through a narrative logic, can reveal why certain narratives gain more traction than others. The paradigm can also suggest an approach to constructing solid strategic communication intended to solicit, manage, or nurture. According to Fisher, a narrative is "good" (and thus participates in the logic of good reasons governing behavior, decisionmaking and sensemaking) when it exhibits two traits: probability and fidelity. Narrative probability is the internal logic to the story system (coherence), while fidelity is whether an audience finds that "the stories they experience ring true with the stories they know to be true."[31] In our view, Fisher's theory applies primarily to narrative as a sense-making process (a cognitive process of understanding). But the principles of coherence and fidelity can apply to the analysis of individual stories (as socio-cultural objects) as well. Therefore, a single video, such as the amateur video "*Ye Qydi Fi sbil allah*" [sic] (Oh prisoners in the path of God),[32] might contain a coherent and familiar narrative arc (the trajectory of actions and events that structure the narrative from its originating conflict and desire through to its resolution).[33] The video depicts scenes of Guantanamo Bay, Cuba, prisoners, mujahideen attacking the U.S. military with IEDs and rocket-propelled grenades (RPGs), and U.S. coffins draped in American flags. The video does not follow a specific individual as the main character or protagonist, but the narrative arc is nevertheless coherent (insurgents fight and kill U.S. soldiers because their brethren have been captured and tortured), and it rings true. By showcasing American coffins (asserting that American soldiers have died), the video builds on the fidelity of past stories of Muslim victory over invading forces.

FORMAL ELEMENTS AND VISUAL WORK

The official videos AQAM produces frequently feature an individual leader (e.g., Zawahiri) or a spokesman (e.g., Adam Gadahn) giving a statement or speech on a particular topic or current event.[34] This trend predates digital online video, when the primary media were VHS tapes or audiocassettes. The feature of the lecture-style address, rooted in the tradition of Friday mosque sermons, is a frequent element of these organizations' videos. The speakers weave stories into these statements and often draw analogies between recent local events and "historical" events that are generally familiar to any Muslim. By presenting the jihad-ist ideologue as the sole speaker in frame, the video positions him as an authority figure, again leveraging the tradition of mosque sermons and madrasa peda-gogy. Famous battles (e.g., Badr) and Muslim heroes (e.g., Saladin) are particularly popular.[35] Often these videos contain footage of operations or training exer-cises, and increasingly, the producers utilize the style of a news program to inform group members and the broader online audience. By following the pattern of news broadcasts, these videos attempt to mask their propagandistic nature. Furthermore, the juxtaposition of visual elements, such as AQAM military training with U.S. coffins, suggests that the United States is a defeatable enemy at the hands of the mujahadeen.[36] Thus, the formal structure and visual elements com-bine to execute an ideological function of the narra-tive, obscuring details that might offer an avenue toward an alternative interpretation.

As AQAM videos have begun to look more like news broadcasts, the mainstream media increasingly use them as source material. As Dauber has noted, "the irony here is that the traditional (*legacy*) Ameri-can media outlets now depend on the terrorists and in-surgents for media content."[37] This situation increases the reach of AQAM propaganda and the prestige and legitimacy of their media output within the contested population. It also further illustrates the blurring be-tween media producers and consumers. Phillip Seib and Dana Janbek's study described terrorist videos as fitting into five broad categories: ideological lectures, interviews, propaganda documentaries, battle scenes, and martyr showcases.[38] Within these formats, we also see the AQAM videos borrowing techniques from the amateur videos, which share traits with the global digital media culture.

A notable formal trait, evident in "*As Sahab Media Lions of Jihad Part 1*," is the incorporation of a video game aesthetic.[39] Utilizing production effects software, these videos incorporate 3D fly-throughs of buildings and landscapes and other animated sequences. This technique serves two functions, as Dauber has noted elsewhere in this volume. First, the logos and fly-through vignettes serve a branding purpose. Second, these elements share much in common with globally popular cultural practices. While these animated sequences might seem highly polished and professional, they actually demonstrate a shared, amateur technique.[40]

The advent of user-friendly, consumer-oriented multimedia software initiated a transformation that is evident in the extremist video genre. Following key trends worldwide, newer extremist videos, and especially "jihobbyist" videos, engage in practices of mashup, remix, and reappropriation.[41] New media's modularity, repeatability, and capacity for transcoding facilitate remix and reappropriation.[42] Whether adding a song to a video or intersplicing Hollywood movie scenes, the practices of remix, mashup, and reappropriation exhibit a bricolage of newly produced content combined with accessible content from popular culture.[43] Widely available software facilitates this work. These features work with a globalized culture industry and the exchange of cultural production between cultural sub-groups.

Exploiting remix culture, the extremist video genre exhibits traits that can communicate across multiple language groups (emphasizing visual storytelling and widely shared formal strategies). One representative example is a video entitled "*Al-Shahada*" that circulated in 2010 (since removed) on *DailyMotion.com*. It displays a typical trope of the mashup extremist video: the use of religious music or Qu'ranic recitation paired with moving images of slain jihadists, placed over an image of a lush green paradise (or *jannah*). Such productions transcend language barriers and also appeal to illiterate individuals. In an ironic display of remix culture, "*Al-Shahada*" borrows from American film productions, including Ridley Scott's *Kingdom of Heaven*, interjecting excerpted scenes next to an al-Qaeda training video, together forging a new narrative. These reappropriations show actors portraying medieval warriors winning battles on horseback and connect viewers to a long history of celebrated warriors for Islam. They activate nostalgia and link contemporary conflicts of the modern day extremists to battles recounted in the annals of Islamic history.

While "*Al-Shahada*" is only one video, it is a content-rich example of an entire genre of videos. These videos share formal characteristics of reappropriated mainstream cultural products juxtaposed with amateur footage, the incorporation of news footage of American bombing campaigns, the application of desktop editing software effects, and the invocation of "heavenly" imagery (clouds, trees, etc.). Other common visual tropes incorporated through the mashup style include images of lions and Arabic calligraphy.[44] Together these formal elements execute a combination of functions. First, by exhibiting the same remix style common throughout global online culture, pro-AQAM videos share much with other popular fan videos circulating online. They are not marginal, at least on a formal basis, but rather familiar. Second, the mashup style's editing patterns, lacking any adherence to continuity editing (the style of American film/ television designed to create consistent story worlds), privileges visual content, especially the visual symbols and the authoritative speakers. Finally, the juxtapositions frame events and the emphasized associations in the video.

CONTENT ELEMENTS AND NARRATIVE WORK

The extremist video genre broadly exhibits a valorization of violence and positions contemporary jihadists as the heirs of heroes in Islamic history. This consistent mythology facilitates the vertical integration of the narrative systems in which these videos participate. "*Al-Shahada*," for example, connects the long-standing narrative tradition of martyrdom (and its rewards) in its valorization of extremists slain for the cause. By juxtaposing the images of these extremists with battle footage from Iraq, Afghanistan, or Chechnya, the video integrates contemporary political conditions with the historical narrative trajectory. Importantly, the integration of the martyrdom narrative activates the personal, because martyrdom is an action available to anybody—even the most disenfranchised youth with few resources or skills can die for the cause.[45] Thus, the historical and contemporary narratives provide an arc that presents a resolution to one's personal narrative trajectory, one that concludes with a reward (valorization, attainment of *jannah* ["lush green paradise"], etc.).

This process of *vertical integration* is an important narrative function executed by the story content of pro-AQAM videos, and is a hallmark of extremist strategic communication.[46] Vertical integration is the process whereby a long-standing cultural embedded narrative or story system integrates a less-developed and previously unrelated story or story system, often

119

of a local event, into itself. For example, AQAM vertically integrated the 2003 American invasion of Iraq into the Tatar narrative for rhetorical and actionable ends.[47] Audiences were encouraged to see alarming parallels between the Tatar invasion of Iraq under Hulagu Khan in the 13th century (and the ensuing bloodshed and destruction) and the American invasion of Iraq under President George W. Bush. In doing so, audiences learned about American intentions in Iraq, the "true" nature of the invasion, and what the response must be. The Mamluks and the Sultan Baybars defeated the fierce Tatars in battle at Ayn Jalut in 1260. The historical narrative of the Tatars and their defeat provides a template for understanding the contemporary moment imbued with coherence (fight the invaders to deliver Muslim lands) and fidelity (a superior invading military force has been defeated by Muslims in the past).[48]

Not only do these videos frequently exhibit vertical integration,[49] but they also participate in populating a narrative landscape with narratives of AQAM as the champions of Islam. While story systems in the United States and the West portray AQAM as villains, videos like *"Tribute to the Lion: Sheikh Osama bin Laden (May Allah Accept Him As A Martyr)"* construct stories of heroic leadership and martyrdom.[50] This video compiles clips of bin Laden in the field leading mujahideen (clips reappropriated from As-Sahab, CNN, and other sources). Similar videos celebrating Abu Musab Al-Zarqawi, Anwar Al-Awlaki, and others establish a consistent pattern within the narrative landscape. Thus, counter-message strategies designed to portray these figures as villains run opposite to the principle of narrative fidelity. While delegitimizing AQAM leaders is important, we recommend messages that sidestep the challenge of achieving fidelity in a narrative landscape in which videos present AQAM leaders as champions.

IMPLICATIONS

Digital Outreach Team.

In the narrative landscape of AQAM and jihobbyist videos, the U.S. State Department finds itself engaged in an information war. The Digital Outreach Team (DOT) is at the center of that effort. Operating on a small budget with a small team of linguists, DOT produces mashup videos for distribution in various online venues. Their budgets, production style, and distribution methods generally mimic those of jihobbyists, not the official media divisions of AQAM (between which an increasingly blurry distinction exists).

In one DOT video, text on screen (in Arabic) narrates the Arab Spring and asks, "Where was Osama bin Laden?"[51] Crickets chirp as the video cuts to an isolated bin Laden wrapped in a blanket watching himself on television with a remote control in his hand. Ridiculing the al-Qaeda leader, DOT attacks the coherence of bin Laden as a relevant champion. The Arab world is revolting without him. This undermines the fidelity of the larger narrative system in which bin Laden represents a heroic Muslim champion. In another DOT video addressing the Arab Spring, excerpts of Abu Yahya al-Libi denouncing democracy as something contrary to Islam mashes with scenes of al-Azhar clerics marching in favor of democratic change and pious Muslim protestors praying in Cairo as the regime's security forces turn fire hoses on them.[52]

Counternarrative.

As the billion dollars spent in the 2012 U.S. election attests, successfully altering audiences' perceptions of someone is extremely difficult. Even when successful, counter-narrative techniques like delegitimization and disruption leave a sense-making gap, with the underlying desire for resolution still present. Recalling the narrative arc that governs most narrative systems, a conflict initiates a desire and a series of actions and participants, which drives toward a resolution. Eliminating a participant such as a champion leaves a gap requiring a new champion; identifying actions as ineffectual leaves a gap requiring new actions. But since the conflict and the other story components remain, the engine of the narrative arc stays in place, leaving other components still driving forward toward resolution.

The Leuprecht study emphasizes the importance of the underlying grievances in the extremist narratives. These grievances are critical because they form the foundation of the conflict or desires that instigate the narrative trajectory of actor/agents and events proceeding toward a resolution. Counter-narratives that successfully eliminate the coherence of an actor/agent (e.g., bin Laden) leave the underlying grievance in place. If a strategic communication campaign counters the messages of AQAM, the underlying grievance, such as conditions in the Palestinian territories, remains. Therefore, in addition to disrupting the narrative systems, we argue that *alternative narratives* are a necessary component to the strategic communication plan.

Alternative Narrative.

The alternative narrative approach acknowledges the legitimacy of a community's grievance(s) (in this case, those of AQAM proponents) and recognizes the source of conflict and desired resolution. However, it also charts a different pathway toward that resolution by other means. This alternative narrative arc emphasizes stories with different participants, actions, and events. In both form and content, the alternative narrative must remain familiar and integrate into the existing narrative landscape, lest the target audience reject it. In short, it must maintain coherence and fidelity.

In the application of the theory, an alternative-narrative video shares the same prevalent motifs as the pro-AQAM videos, namely the mashup style of global remix culture. By incorporating news and film footage, images, and music (especially hip-hop), the video achieves a stylistic familiarity and congruence within the narrative landscape of the contested population. Leveraging hip-hop music is particularly appropriate because of its global popularity and common pairing with ideologically charged image sequences by jihobbyists.[53] By following the patterns of global remix culture and the extremist mashup videos, an alternative-narrative video could address multicultural and transnational target audiences, emphasizing the use of visual storytelling and music.

An alternative narrative strategy begins with understanding the narrative system and its components. The narrative system of the aforementioned "*Al-Shahada*" video exhibits a conflict, namely the oppression of Muslims at the hands of aggressive outside forces. This conflict generates a desire to overcome that oppression. The stories, participants, and events (which are the key components) drive toward a satisfaction of that desire or a resolution of the conflict. The counter-narrative approach, which disrupts a champion, leaves a gap that must be filled to retain coherence and maintain sense-making. The alternative narrative approach addresses the broader narrative logic and fills the narrative gap. It operates within the narrative landscape, integrating into existing narrative systems but in a manner that has alternative ideological implications.

Instead of eliminating AQAM narratives, akin to an artillery unit destroying a mortar emplacement, an alternative-narrative video would exhibit a familiar narrative logic applicable to existing grievances as exploited in extremist narratives. However, the means of resolution would be radically different. The alternative narrative would contain elements that offer a foreseeable resolution to the conflict (coherence), such as a story about a Muslim champion defeating an identifiable threat. The Arab Spring is fertile terrain for alternative narratives. Champions and martyrs abound in this narrative system, with a still-ongoing arc toward resolution of the conflict of oppression.

Similarly, stories of Muslim champions of nonviolence and civil disobedience, such as Abdul Ghaffar Khan (d. 1988), offer valuable opportunities for alternative narratives.[54] In such a narrative system, a foreign colonial occupier (the British Empire) invades and oppresses Muslims, and a champion (Khan) emerges to rally his community in a nonviolent struggle for freedom to defeat the occupiers. As an experiment with the theory of alternative narrative and global remix style, the authors created a short video conveying the narrative of Khan's struggle, mimicking the pattern evident in the jihobbyist videos.[55] However, the Islamic resistance or jihad of Khan and his followers (known as the *"Servants of God"*) was nonviolent, and akin to Mahatma Gandhi's simultaneous efforts in India.

The goal of this alternative narrative is to create a culturally relevant and authentic narrative that does not ignore or dismiss underlying grievances, but offers similar story forms, similar genre conventions, and similar touchstones the visual strategies of the remix style facilitates. Montages of close-up shots of Khan forge an intimacy between the story's hero and the viewer, and images of Khan book-end the grainy newsreel footage, visually communicating that Khan's nonviolent jihad defeated the colonial occupier. Emphasizing the contemporary relevance of Khan's tactics and ideology, a scene transitions a black-and-white image of a Servant of God (coded as "past" like the newsreel) to color, revealing his iconic crimson robes. These visual elements, therefore, are central both to the form (following the patterns of remix style as many extremist videos do) and content, allowing the video the opportunity to circulate in a narrative landscape marked by stories of Muslim heroes, battles against outsiders, and restoration of Islamic identity and dignity.

Public lamentations that the United States is losing the information war have perhaps put too much emphasis on the "war" analogy. This analogy encourages the notion that the right weapon will defeat the enemy in an oppositional relationship. What the theories of dialogism (Bakthin), the narrative paradigm (Fisher), and detailed analysis of visual narratives illustrate is the complex and interrelated nature of communication. Thus, while the propaganda of AQAM and their supporters produce warrant disruption and counter-ing, U.S. strategic communication would benefit from an emphasis on highlighting new and alternative paths through the narrative landscape.

ENDNOTES - CHAPTER 5

1. Joby Warrick, "Clinton: U.S. Losing Global Public Relations Battle—to 'Baywatch' and Wrestling," *The Washington Post*, 2011, available from *www.washingtonpost.com/wp-dyn/content/article/2011/03/02/ AR2011030206898.html*.

2. "Transcript Of Senate Foreign Relations Committee Hearing on the Proposed Fiscal 2012 Foreign Relations Budget," Washington, DC: U.S. Senate, available from *www.foreign.senate.gov*.

3. Cori E. Dauber, for example, has detailed how video production equipment has become as important as traditional arms, and how complicit Western news organizations have unwittingly fomented the extremists' propaganda efforts. See Cori E. Dauber, *YouTube War: Fighting in a World of Cameras in Every Cell Phone and Photoshop on Every Computer*, Carlisle, PA: Strategic Studies Institute, U.S. Army War College, 2009. Philip Seib and Dana Janbek, meanwhile, have provided a wide-ranging survey of digital media use by major terrorist groups, with an emphasis on long-range educational and ideological goals. See Philip Seib and Dana Janbek, *Global Terrorism and New Media: The Post-Al Qaeda Generation*, London, UK, and New York: Routledge, 2010. Jarret Brachman, a leading expert on terrorism, has detailed the propaganda machine of al-Qaeda. See Jarrett Brachman, *Global Jihadism: Theory and Practice*, London, UK, and New York: Routledge, 2008.

4. President of the United States, Executive Order 13584, September 9, 2011, Washington, DC: The White House, available from *www.whitehouse.gov/the-press-office/2011/09/09/executive-order-13584-developing-integrated-strategic-counterterrorism-c*.

5. Secretary of State Clinton should also be recognized for her support and advocacy of the Digital Outreach Team (DOT) and its approach of entering into global conversations via new media.

Our goal here is to suggest an additional dimension to the State Department's efforts.

6. Christian Leuprecht, Todd Hatalay, Sophia Moskalenko, and Clark McCaulay, "Winning the Battle But Losing the War: Narrative and Counter-Narrative Strategy," *Perspectives on Terrorism*, Vol. 3, No. 2, 2009, available from *www.terrorismanalysts.com/ pt/index.php/ pot/article/view/68/html*.

7. See, for example, Gabriel Weimann and Conrad Winn, *The Theater of Terror: Mass Media and International Terrorism*, London, UK: Longman Group, 1993.

8. Coercion and consent are two crucial elements of political theorist Antonio Gramsci's conception of cultural hegemony. His ideas are instructive for the contemporary situation where a combination of kinetic action (coercion) and ideological action (consent) are central for the struggle to earn the right to govern a contested population. For details on ideology, hegemony, and coercion/consent, see Antonio Gramsci, *Selections from the Prison Notebooks*, Quintin Hoare and Geoffrey Nowell Smith, eds. and trans., New York: International Publishers, 1971.

9. See Dauber, *YouTube War*; and Brachman, *Global Jihadism*.

10. By "hegemonic processes," we mean the methods of coercion and consent AQAM pursues in order to exert influence over the population they target. Terrorist acts, videos, and audiocassette statements all participate in these hegemonic processes. For more on hegemonic processes in narrative and communication, see Daniel Bernardi, Pauline Hope Cheong, Chris Lundry, and Scott W. Ruston, *Narrative Landmines: Rumors, Islamist Extremism and the Struggle for Strategic Influence*, Piscataway, NJ: Rutgers University Press, 2012.

11. "Prosumer" is a combination of "producer" and "consumer," expressing the convergence of these two formerly distinct roles within the global media ecology. Advances in technology (and reductions in price), along with forums such as YouTube have spawned a class of global citizens who create as much media content as they watch or read.

12. Brachman, *Global Jihadism,* p. 19. As Brachman further explains on the same page:

> Jihobbyists may do it from the comfort of their home computer or their local coffee shop, but they are still actively seeking to move forward the jihadist agenda [through a variety of means, including website design and propaganda posters].

13. Jarret Brachman, "Al-Qaeda in a Post-Bin Laden World," Speech at Arizona State University, Tempe, AZ, February 23, 2012.

14. *As Sahab Media Lions of Jihad Part 1,* YouTube video. Uploaded by 0tarbix1 on November 1, 2011 (no longer available).

15. The *shahadah* (testimony) is the common Islamic statement of faith that affirms the absolute oneness of God and the prophethood of Muhammad. It is the first of the five pillars in Sunni Islam. Its depiction on banners, flags, and other visual content is popular among AQAM as an affirmation of God's supreme sovereignty over all things, including state governments and international governing bodies. Thus, it can serve as an implicit rejection of non-Islamic ideologies (e.g., communism), state governments, or entities such as The North Atlantic Treaty Organization or the United Nations.

16. This example paraphrased from Story #ONR-SEA0105 in the Center for Strategic Communication, Arizona State University, Tempe, AZ, database of extremist stories.

17. See Jeffry R. Halverson, H. L. Goodall, and Steve R. Corman, *Master Narratives of Islamist Extremism*, New York: Palgrave Macmillan, 2010, pp. 13-26.

18. The Boston Tea Party is another example of narrative as a system. The individual stories of Samuel Adams and the other colonists (including protests in colonies other than Massachusetts) constitute the original narrative system. The narrative accumulated other stories of resistance and tax revolt over time, culminating in the naming of the Tea Party movement in 2010. Thus, what we call the Boston Tea Party is a macro-narrative system with broad historical interrelationships.

19. *Al-Jihad fisabilillah,* available from *www.youtube.com/watch?v=triBDEJPslA.*

20. John Louis Lucaites and Celeste Michelle Condit, "Reconstructing 'equality': Culturaltypal and Counter-Cultural Rhetorics in the Martyred Black Vision," *Communication Monographs,* Vol. 57, March 1990, p. 8.

21. For more on narrative landscapes, their constituent components, and strategic communication, see Bernardi *et al.*

22. Mikhail Bakhtin, *Speech Genres and Other Late Essays,* Vern W. McGee, trans., Austin, TX: University of Texas Press, 1986, p. 91.

23. Tamar Katriel and Aliza Shenhar: "Tower and Stockade: Dialogic Narration in Israeli Settlement Ethos," *The Quarterly Journal of Speech,* Vol. 76, No. 4, 1990, pp. 359-380.

24. W. Lance Bennett and Murray Edelman: "Toward a New Political Narrative," *Journal of Communication,* Vol. 35, No. 4, 1985, p. 161.

25. "نشودة لبيك اسلام البطولة النشخة الكاملة+ لقطات مؤثرة" ("Muslim Heroic Full Song; Emotional Pieces"), available from *www.youtube/2iLvypqkgWU.*

26. "أبكاني كثيرا هذا النشي" ("This Song Made me Cry a Lot"), available from *www.youtube/YfmsIUdzUCY.*

27. Hamzah, a great warrior and uncle of Muhammad, is known as "The Lion of God" and established the lion as a symbol of warrior prowess and piety.

28. *U.S. Army Field Manual, No. 3-24; Marine Corps Warfighting Manual, No. 3-33.5, U.S. Army/Marine Corps Counterinsurgency Manual,* Chicago, IL: University of Chicago Press, 2007, p. 25.

29. See also Jeremy Tambling, *Narrative and Ideology,* Buckingham, UK: Open University Press, 1991; Bernardi *et al.* pp. 7-41; Lucaites and Condit.

30. Walter Fisher, "Narration as a Human Communication Paradigm: The Case of Public Moral Argument," *Communication Monographs*, Vol. 31, March 1984, p. 8.

31. *Ibid.*

32. AMOWAAS, *Ye Qydi Fi sbil allah*, available from *www.youtube.com/watch?v=tGrPHO6Uya4&feature=related*.

33. Narrative theorists from Aristotle to Gustav Freitag to Kenneth Burke have all articulated a similar structure to narrative: a conflict (or a lack) instantiates a desire and the participants of the story take actions and experience events moving toward a resolution of the conflict and satisfaction of the desire.

34. As Dauber's Chap. 6 in this volume explores in detail, great care and attention has been placed on branding organizational videos with a logo.

35. The Battle of Badr and the story of the champion, Saladin, play central roles in Muslim history and identity, and especially the rhetorical strategies of jihadist ideologues. See Halverson, *et al.*, for detailed analyses of these two master narratives, among others frequently leveraged by extremists.

36. See *Ye Qaidi - New 2011 Urdu Nasheed - Ye Qaidy Fi Sabeelillah,* (translation), available from *www.youtube/e8cPjAQkkX4*.

37. Dauber, Chap. 6, p. 22.

38. Seib and Janbek, p. 51.

39. *As Sahab Media Lions of Jihad Part 1,* YouTube video, uploaded by 0tarbix1 on November 1, 2011, (no longer available), accessed on February 1, 2012.

40. "Machinima" is one of many forms of digital video storytelling popular worldwide among amateurs. Machinima creators utilize the game engine of 3D first-person video games to create video sequences of moving through space and acting out scenes, then editing these scenes together using desktop video production software. See *www.machinima.net*.

41. New media and cultural studies scholar Henry Jenkins has tracked the evolution of these practices from their early manifestation by science fiction fans to the global phenomenon evident today. See Henry Jenkins, *Textual Poachers: Television Fans and Participatory Culture*, New York: Routledge, 1992; Henry Jenkins, *Convergence Culture: Where Old and New Media Collide*, New York: New York University Press, 2006.

42. Transcoding is the capacity to transfer digital content from one format into another format. Converting analog cassette tape to 8-track tape is a difficult, time consuming effort. Converting a .wav audio file to a .aiff audio file is a simple and speedy process. See Lev Manovich, *The Language of New Media*, Cambridge, MA: The MIT Press, 2002.

43. Bricolage is an assemblage of elements drawn from whatever is available. The term is more commonly applied to moving image, and differs from "collage" in its connotation of random selection of components from immediately available sources.

44. For examples, see "أبكاني كثيرا هذا النشيد," available from www.youtube/YfmsIUdzUCY, accessed on December 12, 2012.; "Jihad Nasheed," available from *www.youtube.com/watch? v=D cdQxCCnhOU&feature=share&list= PLEF3BF603D7D70093*, accessed on December 12, 2012.; "انشودة جلجلت؛ترفع من متك ذابن هلله," available from *www.youtube/Zo4G_jt_QLE*, accessed on December 17, 2012.; " القولا لقول الصوارم) لا أبا وبأ علي ..!, | ~ | أنشودة)" available from *www.youtube/wlRK4yFWGx8*, accessed on December 17, 2012.; "ARABIC JIHAD NASHEED رائع نشيد عن الجهاد," available from *www.youtube/2i2n2JY410I*, accessed on December 17, 2012.; "(Jihad Nasheed) Anjooma Layat," available from *www.youtube/ lxo9iEX8W1c*, accessed on December 17, 2012.; "Nasheed Jihad wal Fida," available from *www.youtube.com/ watch?v=qPJg3WL rsBw&feature=share&list=ULqPJg3WLrsBw*, accessed December 17, 2012.

45. For a detailed account of martyr master narratives, personal actions, and vertical integration, see Jeffry R. Halverson, Scott W. Ruston, and Angela Trethewey, "Mediated Martyrs of the Arab Spring: New Media, Civil Religion and Narrative in Egypt and Tunisia" Unpublished Manuscript, 2013.

46. For a detailed account of extremist strategic communication and vertical integration, see Halverson, Goodall, and Corman.

47. The well-known characterization of the Iraq War as a reincarnation of the Crusades, which expanded to characterize the entirety of the U.S. "war on terror," illustrates the multiscalar and mutable nature of narrative understanding. The Tatar narrative applies very specifically to Iraq, since the 13th century Tatars invaded and destroyed Baghdad. At the time of the invasion, Zawahiri likened Bush to Tatar leader Hulagu Khan. The American alliance with Shiite leaders also fit the historical template as Khan was aided by a Shiite representative.

48. For more on vertical integration as well as the Tatar narrative, see Halverson, Goodall, and Corman; see also David Betz, "The Virtual Dimension of Insurgency and Counter-Insurgency," *Small Wars and Insurgencies*, Vol. 19, No. 4, December 2008, pp. 510-540.

49. Vertical integration is closely related to narrative coherence and fidelity. The story forms and archetypes that are part of narrative systems provide structure for subsequent stories and thus facilitate coherence. Vertically integrated stories inherently exhibit narrative fidelity. The long-standing cultural narratives (or "master narratives") participate in the establishment of a culture's identity and values and thus are the basis of that which "rings true" (to use Fisher's terms). For strategic communicators concerned about messages not ringing true in a culture, they would be wise to investigate that culture's master narratives in order to craft a message strategy consistent with those master narratives.

50. Tribute to the Lion, available from *www.youtube.com/watch?v=c_ePYdPYfrw*, accessed on October 26, 2012.

51. "الشعوب العربية تنتفض، لكن أين أسامة بن لادن؟", ("Arab peoples Rebelled, But Where Is Osama Bin Laden?)," YouTube video uploaded by the State Department, available from *www.youtube.com/watch?v=W0TkpBYDZ3Y &feature=plcp*, accessed June 28, 2012.

52."القاعدة: الديمقراطية هي العدو ", ("Al Qaeda: Democracy Is the Enemy"), YouTube video, uploaded by the State Department, available from *www.youtube.com/watch?v=6rD0551S8RQ&feature= plcp,* accessed June 28, 2012.

53. In addition, hip-hop exhibits at least a rudimentary alignment with traditional Islamic art forms that are acceptable to extremists and hard-liners, namely poetry and percussion. Furthermore, since hip-hop was born among disenfranchised African Americans seeking redress for grievances against U.S. society, its use carries a degree of fidelity in a narrative landscape dominated by distrust of American hegemony.

54. See Jeffry R. Halverson, *Searching for a King: Muslim Nonviolence and the Future of Islam,* Washington, DC: Potomac Books, 2012.

55. "Voices for Non-Violence in the Muslim World Symposium," Symposium video, Arizona State University, Tempe, AZ, October 22, 2010.

SECTION III:

PERSPECTIVES ON AUDIENCES AND
IMAGES IN ONLINE ENVIRONMENTS

CHAPTER 6

THE BRANDING OF VIOLENT JIHADISM

Cori E. Dauber

At the end of the 20th century, al-Qaeda was more or less a cohesive organization that existed in the physical world, even if it had critical interrelationships with other like-minded organizations. With the loss of its physical bases in Afghanistan after the September 11, 2001 attacks, however, the organization had to adapt to new circumstances. It did so partly through its well-documented transformation to a largely online entity, and when it did so, the original group—whether you call it "al-Qaeda Central," "al-Qaeda Prime," "al-Qaeda 1.0" or anything else—became less and less important as a specific group of people who were themselves threatening the West. Simultaneously, however, the core group of individuals became more important as the center of a network of groups all gaining inspiration and, to some extent, identity, from their association with that original group. In short, al-Qaeda shifted from being a specific and identifiable terrorist group to being a *brand*.

Several of the groups linked with the al-Qaeda "brand" have been conscious that they were adopting a brand (that is, *an identity*) as a specific group of individuals. When abu Musab al-Zarqawi, the leader of "al-Qaeda in Iraq,"[1] was deciding whether to associate his group with al-Qaeda, he "began to think in business terms. A merger with al-Qaeda, he thought, would give him the option of tapping into more fighters, more money, and *greater brand recognition*."[2] Other evidence confirms that al-Qaeda's affiliate groups concerned themselves with the strength of that brand over time. Certainly, the surviving members of the original al-Qaeda organization developed particular concerns about "brand identity," as it was one of the topics of Osama bin Laden and his subordinates hiding in Abbottabad.[3] This development—terrorist group as brand identity—makes sense. Once al-Qaeda in its original form lost the sanctuary of Afghanistan after the American invasion in 2001 and had to reimagine itself as a social movement, (as much ideology and online presence as physical organization), its brand identity became central to its very existence. One key implication of the change took place when "al Qaida . . . transformed from a terrorist organization that selectively leverages the media to advance its objectives into a media organization that selectively leverages terrorism to advance its objectives."[4]

In this chapter, I will look explicitly at the way al-Qaeda and affiliated movements (AQAM) have built brand identity *visually*, in the same way Western corporations have: through the use of often elaborately designed logos. I will do so by looking at the logos burned onto the propaganda videos AQAM groups have produced and by applying the research findings available in the business and marketing literature studying corporate logos. Additionally, many videos start with several seconds of computer animated graphics. Because AQAM groups have used these animated sections for years and because group logos are often central characters in these animated shorts, I will also consider them at length in this chapter.[5]

To be clear, this initial research on AQAMs' use of logos is not based on a random sample. This chapter will concentrate on logos drawn from three sources:

1. *IntelCenter Terrorist and Rebel Logo Identification Guide;*[6]

2. A selection from the author's collection used to fill certain key gaps (for example, IntelCenter did not include any Chechen/Kavkas groups[7]);

3. A selection from the author's collection of media distribution or production wings of large terrorist groups. Those media departments often have their own logo distinct from that of the group proper and their logos were included as well.[8]

My approach will be to survey the literature available on branding and logos, attempt to determine which results are likely to be culture bound and which universal, and then, based on that literature, analyze the logos of these groups.

THE ROLE OF LOGOS IN AQAM VIDEOS

Terrorist groups generally, and AQAM specifically, almost all have some sort of unique identifying logo. This, too, makes sense, for as "part of a graphic identity system, a logo serves as a tangible cue for brand image."[9] Logos have become a standard feature of AQAM and other violent jihadist groups' videos over the last few years, certainly since the height of the Iraq war. Most include sophisticated designs, with multiple design components and symbolic value for their target audiences.

Logos function similarly for violent jihadist groups as they do for corporations. A "logo may be defined as the official visual representation of a corporate or brand name, and the essential component of all corporate and brand identity programs. Its importance derives not from any intrinsic quality . . . but from its ubiquity."[10]

Logos in the videos these groups produce signal followers to trust the authenticity of the group's product. Logos are symbols that function as an "efficient management tool to orchestrate the desired features that the organization wants to express towards its stakeholders."[11] Most involve elaborate designs, with multiple design components, most of which have symbolic value.

Many groups' videos include an image of their logo burned on, which remains throughout the video. The visual strategy is reminiscent of that professional news networks use, but the logos are more visible, since broadcast networks attempt to make their logos simultaneously visible (to ensure the network receives credit for the story through all rebroadcasts) yet inconspicuous (to avoid detracting from the story itself). Broadcast news logos are thus gray-scale, small, and tend toward the translucent. The logos of AQAM (and, during the war in Iraq, Iraqi insurgent groups), by comparison, are high contrast, as they are full color, opaque, and often relatively large.

AQAMs' history with video production is worth noting here. Initially, AQAM used a "building block system" to produce videos during the Iraq war. As Daniel Kimmage and Kathleen Rudolfo describe, the system was simple and efficient:

> In the case of short attack videos, only the footage of the actual attack need come from Iraq. Once an affiliated individual has received that footage and basic accompanying information, which can be transferred over the Internet or by mobile phone, he has only to add the insurgent group's logo, a short title sequence, and perhaps a soundtrack with a motivational song. He then uploads the resulting video product to a free upload-download site and posts an announcement

to a forum. The video-editing software required to produce such a video is cheap and readily available. More importantly, the only material needed from Iraq is the actual footage of the attack. All of the additional elements required to create a video clip—insurgent group logo, songs, etc.—are readily available on the Internet. . . .[12]

In a context where enormous opportunities to generate the type of footage desired for these videos existed, for the first time, the technologies became available to make it possible to film, edit, and upload video clips of attacks in individual segments—even if they were only a few seconds long. Yet, the skill and hardware (and probably software) needed to take full advantage of such clips was not available in the same geographic areas generating the clips, at least not initially.[13]

Once those clips appeared on the web, however, they were available to anyone. At this point, the extremist groups Jarret Brachman labeled "jihobbyists" stepped in and began using the clips to make their own videos in support of the movement.[14] Such freelancing was not surprising. After all, al-Qaeda leaders had emphasized the value of "media jihad" to their followers for some time, and the need for them to make whatever contribution they could, from wherever they could, even if that contribution did not involve their joining the fight directly. Given the opportunity, followers were under the impression that they would be expected to take advantage of it. The result was a flood of "jihobbyists" who indeed took advantage, producing videos of their own.[15]

Rather than be grateful to the jihobbyists for the direct support of their media campaign, jihadist leaders became concerned that the influx of material from unknown and uncontrolled sources would create ideological confusion on a grand scale for the masses. Distinctions between groups, and the basis for fights between them, were, after all, incredibly nuanced. The result was warnings, such as those published in October 2006, that "the ease of internet-based media production is a threat to the credibility and authority of jihadist — and, by analogy, insurgent — media."[16] The online environment made it too easy for too many to create the media products that leaders had touted as a legitimate and important way to "wage jihad." The imprimatur of the al-Qaeda brand was being put at risk.

In response, groups began using logos to preserve their brands. The logos helped ensure audiences that al-Qaeda or associated groups had authorized or "blessed" a particular media product. Explicitly, the logos ensured a group's ability to communicate the authenticity and thus the ideological trustworthiness of particular videos directly to followers. Implicitly, they helped groups gain the credit they deserved for their own operations, as each operation received an immediate "brand" before any other group could move in and claim credit. As a result, logos became an essential tool that groups, even the smallest ones, almost never left out of their videos.

THE SCHOLARSHIP OF LOGOS

A substantial literature exists on the impact of logo design on brand loyalty and the way affect transfers from the logo to the brand. Contrary to what one would naturally assume, people do not necessarily transfer their positive feelings about a brand to a logo. Rather, *they transfer their positive (or negative) feelings about a logo to the way they feel about the brand.*[17] Further, the design elements contribute to the way people will feel about a logo. Thus, logos of terrorist groups, particularly AQAM groups, function as a central element of their visual persuasion strategies, as theorists in the field of design management explain:

> [The] reputation a corporation or brand enjoys — its "image" and "positioning" in communication jargon — is more than a matter of visual impression. A positive image and distinctive position is created over time by providing desirable products or services and communicating consistently and effectively. While a logo is just one component of that image, it is the one that identifies the others, operating like a flag. Logic tells us that a flag should invoke respect by virtue of the entity it represents, not by its coloration or pattern. Yet, despite logic, we are all swayed — irrationally, perhaps, but most assuredly — by appearances.[18]

In one study, in fact, respondents reacted differently 55 percent of the time when researchers compared their response to logos alone, with the way they responded to the company name alone without the logo.[19]

Logos function as a visual identifier organizations use to build brand loyalty by strengthening recall of positive associations.[20] Empirical research strongly suggests if viewers like a logo, they transfer those positive feelings to the brand associated with it. Likewise, negative feelings about a logo can lead to an even more intense affect transferring to the brand.[21]

Perhaps the strongest circumstantial evidence for the strength of this relationship is that U.S. companies often spend as much as 20 times more on "permanent media" (signage and so forth) than on advertising.[22]

Nonprofits as well need to create brand loyalty and positive feelings toward their organizations. For a nonprofit group:

> When well designed, a logo is felt to have positive influence on fund raising, corporate sponsorship, merchandise sales, patron subscriptions, brand loyalty, good will, employee morale, and volunteer recruitment. . . .[23]

A consensus has been reached in the scholarly literature that the most effective logos work if viewers remember having seen them (termed "recognition") and if the logo reminds viewers of the correct brand (termed "recall"). Since corporate leaders want audiences to remember their institutions, a logo functions as visual shorthand for companies, or it is not working.[24]

The research literature also concludes that successful logos tend to have several design elements in common. First is "naturalness," meaning items from the physical world are incorporated. Second, they tend to be only moderately elaborate. A logo that is either too elaborate or not elaborate enough will not succeed. The final element is "harmony," a function of symmetry and balance.[25]

Nonabstract symbols (those which are obviously recognizable from the real world, even if highly stylized) appear in the most successful logos. In Western corporate logos, these items include such symbols as Prudential's rock, Wendy's little girl, or Jaguar's cat.[26] For AQAM groups, the parallel would be the pictograms of the Qu'ran, rifles, banners, and other recognizable—and symbolically weighted—items that reappear repeatedly.

A group with limited resources needs the ability to elicit a reaction quickly when it lacks the ability to create multiple exposures to its logo. A group in such a situation has the option of turning to "false recognition," a sense of familiarity when the audience has never before seen a logo. In the United States, companies with low budgets attempt this strategy when they need to have an impact based on initial views of their logo because they cannot afford to build audience response through elaborate promotional campaigns or repeated viewings. Companies in such a situation attempt to create a sense of familiarity in the audience from the very first viewings. This can be accomplished through use of certain design elements. False recognition would depend on design characteristics that would make logos less distinctive from other logos. That would mean less "naturalness, high harmony, multiple parallel lines, and ideally a proportion of a height 75-80% of width."[27]

The ability to produce a terrorist or insurgent propaganda campaign results in the target audiences' ability to recognize a logo when they see it (and recall what it references) depends most of all upon a group's resources, as audience response is built over multiple exposures. This is referred to as "true recognition."

Notably, false recognition is different from brand confusion. False recognition, which is a calculated strategy, is the sense of familiarity that accrues to a logo after an elaborate branding campaign. The point is to elicit that sense even though the particular logo has never actually been looked at before. It can be intentionally evoked through the use of some very specific design strategies. None of those strategies are at play in the case of brand confusion. That is what happens when logos meant to be unique and compelling are simply so close to those of their competitors that audiences have difficulty distinguishing one from the other. They undermine the entire point of the campaigns built around the logos. Brand confusion is the mark of failed or failing marketing campaigns; false recognition may well be a central component of a marketing campaign.[28]

AQAM DESIGN ELEMENTS

The research findings from the business and marketing literature have direct applicability to the design characteristics of logos on AQAM videos. Certain design elements and categories of design elements appear on those logos consistently, and are noteworthy because they reflect research findings about what kind of logo will or will not be effective.

Successful logos incorporate natural design elements, and are moderately elaborate. These findings are reflected in AQAM logos over and over. The groups, in other words, tend to use pictograms that are not simply recognizable representations of items from the physical world, but ones that have strong symbolic value as well. The Qu'ran is illustrative: It is not only a real item from the physical world, but an object that carries strong weight with intended viewers. If logos used just *any* physical item, they would not be very likely to succeed. Instead, they should be items with a deeper meaning for a target audience.

First and foremost among the nonabstract elements appearing in the AQAM logos examined was the Qu'ran. The Qu'ran, of course, sets the Islamist groups apart from all others. For example, the image of the Islamic holy book never appears in visual materials related to Irish or Basque nationalism. The Qu'ran symbolizes the religious motivation for their fight. It also represents the belief of these groups' members that what they do is Islamically justified.

Second in frequency of appearance was some type of weapon. The logos almost always include a weapon, and almost always that weapon was an AK-47. Groups whose logos incorporate a rifle include the 1920 Revolutionary Brigades, Iraq's Jihadist Leagues, Islamic Army in Iraq, Islamic Movement for Iraq's Mujahideen, al-Qaeda in the Land of Islamic Maghreb, Al Madinah al Munawarah Brigades, Jaish al Fatiheen, and the Islamic State of Iraq.[29] AQAM logos demonstrate a clear preference for the AK-47 over the rocket-propelled grenade (RPG) as their iconic weapon. As ubiquitous as the RPG may have been over the last several years, it was never and is not now a weapon present in large enough numbers to be in the hands of every fighter; the AK-47 was and is. The AK-47 is the modern visualization of "by the Sword," as such, it appears rather than actual swords.[30] It stands for the willingness to fight, the need to fight, and the fight itself, as well as the unseen warrior who wields the weapon. Frequently, the logos show the weapon with the arm or hand that grasps or wields it. Only the hand or arm appears in the logo, not the entire fighter. Groups whose logos incorporate a hand or arm include: the 1920 Revolutionary Brigades (a single hand grasping an AK-47), Iraq's Jihadist Leagues (a hand only, holding a Qu'ran), and Jaish al Fatiheeh (arm crossed with rifle).[31] The hand becomes a symbol representative of any fighter, past or future. On the other hand, the only face or head in the groups examined in this chapter appears highly stylized and abstract: The Islamic Army in Iraq uses an image somewhere between a medieval Knight and Darth Vader. The preference for the hand over the head occurs because the head (inevitably, therefore, the face) is specific and unique. The face, of course, is also the locus of the way we distinguish one individual from another, while the hand is a much easier way to symbolize the idea of universality – every fighter is any fighter.[32]

The genius of these logos is that they create more powerful symbols by creating associations between physical items that had symbolic power individually, but now are merged through their proximity within the logo. For example, the Qu'ran has one set of symbolic meanings. An AK-47 or sword has another. Placed together, the two create something new and more powerful than either on its own. With each added symbol, the logo has the potential to become more powerful, as each new association adds another layer of symbolic complexity. While the additions may at first appear to be making a small difference in any given case, either the Qu'ran or a weapon alone is different than the image of the Qu'ran *in combination with* a weapon. This makes sense since the logo is the visualization of a group's identity, and a weapon alone is a tool, not an identity. Only in combination with something else that provides the justification for its use can a weapon provide visualization for a group identity.

This combination of the holy book and a weapon is distinct from the holy book alone – it makes the argument as clearly as it can be made through the use of visual symbols that Islam justifies, indeed mandates, the fight. Followers are not only fighting to defend Islam, they are also fighting because they do not have another choice. Indeed, a central ideological principle for a number of these groups is that jihad – not peaceful, internal struggle, but war – is a central pillar of Islam. That this is not a correct interpretation of the

Islamic faith is well known, as these groups are essentially adding, of their own accord, an additional pillar to the central pillars of Islam.

It is important to consider individual items in isolation, as well. Many (especially insurgent) groups incorporate the map or outline of specific countries into their logos. Iraqi groups do this with the map of Iraq, for example. Otherwise, a number of groups incorporate the map of Palestine or recognizable landmarks from Palestine onto their logo.[33] This approach is actually somewhat of a contradiction. Within Sunni Salafist ideology, nationalism — the loyalty to a specific nation-state — is a very serious theological mistake, given the goal for the entire Muslim world to unify ultimately as one political and religious entity. Where flags or pennants do appear in logos, they are typically variants on "al-raya" the black battle flag of Islam. According to the study produced by West Point's *Combating Terrorism Center*:

> The Black Flag (*al-raya*) traces its roots to the very beginning of Islam. It was the battle (*jihad*) flag of the Prophet Muhammad, carried into battle by many of his companions . . .[t]he flag regained prominence in the 8th century with its use by the leader of the Abbasid revolution, Abu Muslim, who led a revolt against the Umayyid clan and its Caliphate . . . Since then, the image of the black flag has been used as a symbol of religious revolt and battle (i.e. jihad).[34]

The risk for these groups is brand confusion. Consider the clearly differentiated logos of the fast food industry: McDonald's has its arches (and uses a clown), Burger King has a King, and Wendy's has a little girl. But jihadist groups, in competition at the very least for recruits and donors, repetitively use the same symbols over and over, if in slightly different shapes, sizes, colors, and orientations. Many of their logos are not clearly distinguishable from one another, and therefore are not creating a clear visual identity that sets one group apart from the next.

The obvious exception in terms of basic design structure is As-Sahab, the media distribution arm of al-Qaeda central, and likely the most recognizable brand of the entire AQAM media system. As-Sahab's logo is, of course, Arabic lettering that is highly stylized and clearly intended for aesthetic purposes related to branding, not as text per se. There is nothing representational to the logo at all; it is nothing more than the stylized text. However, the finding that representational logos are typically more successful does not mean that *only* representational logos are successful.[35]

The best example of false recognition, the elaborate branding strategy based on the creation of a false sense of familiarity, may be the similarity in basic design between the logo of As-Sahab and that of the relative newcomer, the *al Kataib News Network*. *Al Kataib* is supposedly the media distribution arm of Shabaab, the Somali al-Qaeda affiliate. The logos of these two stand out from those of the majority of groups, because instead of relying on a variety of pictograms that are highly representative, both build on highly stylized and abstract Arabic script. Both Sahab and Kataib, in fact, seem to meet the criteria for "false recognition" with great precision: they are not representational, they include multiple parallel lines, and they are almost—but not quite—as high as they are wide.

While the intent behind the development of the AQAM logo designs is unknowable, no question remains that one after another, the most prominent and repetitive design elements of AQAM logos are those that are mentioned specifically in the business and marketing literature as being successful and effective. Given the potential importance of logos as a central feature of a visual persuasion strategy, focusing on them specifically and understanding how exactly it is they work, alone and as part of a broader visual strategy, is important.

AQAM ANIMATED SHORTS

Animated shorts[36] are not in every video produced by an AQAM group or an independent supporter, not even in a majority of those videos, but they do appear frequently enough and are striking enough to be worthy of some discussion. To be sure, extremist groups employ a wide range in the quality and degree of technical sophistication characterizing these graphics. Some of the shorts are obviously produced using software packages available with the average laptop. The *Al Kataib News Network* videos, supposedly the product of al Shabaab (al-Qaeda's Somali affiliate) always begin with animations lasting as long as 60 seconds and which are clearly the product of a professional media lab. The possibility of such a lab operating somewhere in Somalia remains, but it seems more likely that the group is outsourcing at least a portion of the post production for these videos.[37] Media producers for these groups emphasize logos in many of the shorts and feature them prominently by placing them at the beginning of the videos. The shorts use attention-grabbing graphics, including particularly vibrant colors, notable given that despite how high the production values of these videos are, they tend to feature very low quality footage, grainy, tending toward gray-scale.

Video producers do not feature that type of material by accident—viewers have been trained to "read" that type of footage as "authentic." Cell phone camera footage has become the genuine marker of the real, unedited, nondoctored, image-as-witness. While low grade, poor quality, gray scale footage may have the most credibility; however, it does not necessarily stand out with the groups' target audience. The groups need to initially grab the viewers' attention and have them decide to view the entirety of the video to get out their full message. Given the age level of the target demographic and their short attention span for media materials, many are going to decide whether or not to stick with a video very quickly. In fact, empirical studies indicate viewers may decide whether or not to click through static web sites within 50 *milliseconds*.[38] Therefore, these early mini-movies embedded within the videos may likely make a difference in the viewer's initial decision whether or not to watch the entire video.

AQAM groups vary widely as to the degree of sophistication in their shorts. Yet interestingly, the shorts are no predictor of the video to follow. The most sophisticated short may precede a very primitive video, while a short clearly produced by a "guy-with-a-laptop" may precede the most sophisticated videos in circulation. At the low end, these shorts are very simple, with few colors, few objects, and little movement. In the middle of the continuum are extremely sophisticated animations that, still, were clearly done using animation programs available on individual computers. Sahab's shorts fall into this middle category. On the high end are clearly products of a professional media lab, such as *al Kataib* and *Kavkaz TV*; in such cases, the shorts are really essentially graphics packages.

The animated shorts likely work in concert with the logos. They not only give the logos even more visual prominence than they would have within the videos without the animations, they are a subtle way of claiming legitimacy for the media committees and organizations of these groups. Eye grabbing and flashy as they are, the shorts in many cases clearly mimic the style and format of the introductory sequences of professional news shows.[39] These animations are a way of visually arguing that the organizations producing the videos in which they appear are both ideologically safe and as professional as any other news source. Indeed, they are an appropriate alternative news source for those who do not trust the professional media. For those still unsure whether to affiliate with the movement, the impression left is that such professionalism might translate as trustworthiness and credibility in the video content to follow. After all, in October 2006:

> Al-Boraq released a much-quoted essay on jihadist media titled *Media Exuberance*; the essay warns that jihadists must create legitimate authoritative 'brands' to release media products that can compete with the offerings of mainstream media such as *Al-Jazeera* and *CNN*.[40]

Scholars are not reading into jihadist media products anything that was not quite consciously built in.

CONCLUSIONS

AQAM groups use logos as a critical element of their overall visual strategy. The design elements that appear repeatedly in their logos are those that one finds in the most effective Western branding strategies. Logos are worth examining separately from other aspects of AQAM visual strategy because of the other research finding taken from the study of Western corporate logos: People do not transfer their feelings about a brand to a logo, they transfer their feelings about a logo to a brand. Thus creating a logo that creates positive feelings is a powerful and important visual strategy for any organization.

The business literature used here as a proxy for empirical research on topic does not alter the need for dedicated research involving the target demographics for these groups, both in the English-speaking West and in the Middle East and North Africa (MENA) region. Despite the necessity of finding a starting point for the conduct of empirical research, the military should view the application of findings from the business literature with extreme caution.

Examining the business literature and the solutions offered based on that literature and simply assuming they are appropriate for counter-programming terrorist propaganda would be a mistake. Nevertheless, on a limited set of specific points — for example, the way audiences process and interpret very specific types of visual images — the literature may provide valuable insights. Unlike other special effects, themes, and motifs that appear haphazardly, logos are nearly universally present in jihadist visual products. Useful analytical work is still possible without empirical research, given the available body of research on the use of logos as attempts at visual persuasion. While the conclusions of some of that work is clearly culture bound and not generalizable (for example, making assumptions about the audiences' interpretations of particular symbols), much of it is not, (for example, speaking to the effectiveness of representational symbols, or the most effective proportion for logos). The way a design element is proportioned, height vs. width has to do with the way the eye processes information which would apply in a similar fashion across cultures.[41]

Still, it would be of enormous help to have access to research on the way the target demographic for these groups responded to these particular visual images (and even more helpful if comparative data existed on the way Western and non-Western audiences responded). Obviously AQAM believes that these logos give their media products additional credibility, and based on the available research, they are making all the right design choices for that to be true. Still, the only way to know for sure would be empirical data that is more on point.

ENDNOTES - CHAPTER 6

1. Indeed, people forget that before Zarqawi formally associated with bin Laden, he changed the name of his group from "Tawhid and Jihad" to "Al-Qaeda in Iraq" precisely because of the branding benefits that attached to the name.

2. Seth G. Jones, *Hunting In the Shadows: The Pursuit of Al Qa'ida Since 9/11*, New York: W. W. Norton & Company, 2012, p. 152, [emphasis mine].

3. David Ignatius, "The Plot to Kill President Obama," *Washington Post*, March 16, 2012, available from *www.washingtonpost. com/opinions/the-bin-laden-plot-to-kill-president-obama/2012/03/16/ gIQAwN5RGS_story_1.html*.

4. Jarret Brachman, "Statement before the House Armed Services Committee Subcommittee on Terrorism, Unconventional Threats and Capabilities, on the Topic of Understanding Cyberspace as a Medium for Radicalization and Counter-Radicalization," Washington, DC: U.S. House of Representatives, December 16, 2009, p. 3.

5. For example, As-Sahab, al-Qaeda Central's media distribution arm, has used an animation where (after the Sahab logo

appears, taking up most of the screen, and seems to rotate three-dimensionally) missiles fire and then explode onto an outline of the United States, colored as if an American flag stretched over the entire country. The United States disappears in a giant fireball, at which point the missiles magically reload and fire again, again destroying the United States. Arabic words (still part of the animation) appear in the upper right hand corner of the screen, with actual photographic imagery of an explosion integrated into the image. This animation, used at least as early as 2007, continues to appear on new videos today.

6. Videos examined here were those with a focus on terrorist groups that are jihadist, non-secular, not primarily nationalist in focus, and have recently continued to be active in the production of videos. IntelCenter, *IntelCenter Terrorist and Rebel Logo Identification Guide*, Alexandria, VA: Tempest Publishing, LLC., 2008.

7. The videos of these groups and their supporters have a tendency to appear and disappear with no particular warning. The most important step in research and analysis of this material is to secure it in a permanent form. I download any relevant video in .flv format, and they are available upon request.

8. Hanna Rogan describes many of these groups and their relationships to the larger jihadist network. See Hanna Rogan, *Al-Qaeda's Online Media Strategies: From abu Reuter to Irhabi 007*, FFI-rapport 2007/02729, Kjeller, Norway: Norwegian Defense Research Establishment, January 12, 2007. Although she describes a number of visual texts, she never analyses them as visuals per se, nor does she discuss their use of logos.

9. Marla Royne Stafford, Carolyn Tripp, and Carol C. Bienstock: "The Influence of Advertising Logo Characteristics on Audience Perceptions of a Nonprofit Theatrical Organization," *Journal of Current Issues and Research in Advertising*, Vol. 26, No. 1, Spring 2004, p. 37.

10. As the author continues, it is the single most pervasive element in corporate and brand communications, repeated in every conceivable medium from trucks and signage to packaging and advertising. It represents a continuing, cumulative investment that influences the perceived value of everything that it

touches. Alvin H. Schechter, "Measuring the Value of Corporate and Brand Logos," *Design Management Journal,* Winter 1993, p. 33.

11. Cees B. M. van Riel and Anouschka van den Ban, in cooperation with Evert-Jan Heijmans, "The Added Value of Corporate Logos: An Empirical Study," *European Journal of Marketing,* Vol. 35, No. 3-4, 2001, p. 428.

12. Daniel Kimmage and Kathleen Rudlolfo, *Iraqi Insurgent Media: The War of Images and Ideas*, Washington, DC: Radio Free Europe/Radio Liberty, 2007, p. 35.

13. To be sure, their capabilities in this area over the course of the war improved. See Cori E. Dauber, *YouTube War: Fighting in a World of Cameras in Every Cell Phone, Photo Shop on Every Computer*, Carlisle, PA: Strategic Studies Institute, U.S. Army War College, 2009, p. 16.

14. He explains the term in Jarret M. Brachman, *Global Jihadism: Theory and Practice*, New York: Routledge, 2009, pp. 18-19.

15. As one example of a document widely distributed and which received a great deal of attention, see, *39 Ways to Serve and Participate in Jihad,* translated and posted on *Lauramansfield.com.* The document provides a list of 39 ways individuals can assist the fight, but it heavily emphasizes "helping" by participating in the media jihad (or "e-jihad.") See in particular:

> 12. Praising the Mujahidin, Commemorating Their Exploits, and Urging Others To Follow in Their Footsteps; . . .16 Urging People To Engage in Jihad. What? is very important. If someone is unable to engage in jihad, he must encourage others to do so. The verse in the Koran is: 'Then fight in Allah's cause—Thou art held responsible only for thyself—and rouse the believers' [4:84](30). Another verse states: 'O Messenger, rouse the Believers to the fight' [8:65](31). This obligation extends to both the able-bodied and the impaired. Each Muslim must encourage his brothers to fight the atheists. This is our most pressing need at this time. We must put these verses into practice, for they entail a great reward. The prophet said, 'Whoever has shown the way to good deeds receives a reward *as though he has performed good deeds.'*(32); [My emphasis] . . . 21. Following and Distributing News of

the Jihad . . . The many benefits of this include: . . . * It breaks the media blockade around the community. The enemies have gained control of most media outlets, and they broadcast only what they want. At attempt to spread news of the mujahidin provides the mujahidin with a popular base of media support. * It sows optimism among the community so that Muslims know that the path of pride and dignity lies through jihad and martyrdom. Other methods include: * Forums and chat in the Internet. * Printing out news and distributing it to scholars, students, preachers, and imams to exert a positive influence on them. . . . *Beware of the devil's tricks, which suggest that the distribution of news is a partial measure that does not merit the risk. . . ."* [my emphasis].

The author also speaks at length about the Internet at:

Electronic Jihad: This term has gained widespread usage to describe those who help the jihad through the Internet. This is a blessed medium that benefits us greatly by making it possible for people to distribute and follow the news. It also allows us to defend the mujahidin and publicize their ideas and goals.

This also roughly parallels the time when, according to Brachman, those same "jihobbyists" were moving their attention from reading lengthy ideological tomes to watching (and producing) bloody online videos. See Jarret Brachman, "The Jihad Hobbyists Who've Moved On From Watching Videos," *The Guardian*, February 3, 2012, available from *www.guardian.co.uk/commentisfree/2012/feb/03/jihad-hobbyists-al-qaida*.

16. Kimmage and Rudlolfo, p. 45.

17. Many management experts in the corporate world believe that logos make a difference. In 1994, for example, American companies spent $120,000,000 on creating and deploying new logos. See van Riel and van den Ban, in cooperation with Heijmans, p. 428.

18. Schechter, p. 33.

19. *Ibid.*, p. 35.

20. Much of this research appears in the business literature. Applying that literature to this context, I believe, is appropriate, but only up to a point, which I address in the conclusions.

21. Some authors argue that logos have both intrinsic and extrinsic properties: intrinsic properties are those that have to do with the logo itself, essentially questions of design. Extrinsic properties are those arising from "associations with the company behind the logo . . . partly defined by the behavior of an organization in the past . . ." See van Riel and van den Ban, in cooperation with Heijmans, p. 430. In the nonprofit sector, there is evidence this happened in the cases of the Chicago Symphony Orchestra, and Habitat for Humanity. See Stafford, Tripp, and Bienstock, p. 39.

22. Pamela W. Henderson and Joseph A. Cote, "Guidelines for Selecting or Modifying Logos," *Journal of Marketing*, Vol. 62, April 1998, p. 14.

23. Nonprofits need to think about specific target audiences in logo design, most especially donors and volunteers. Stafford, Tripp, and Bienstock, p. 37. The parallel to terrorist groups, which use their propaganda for fund raising and recruiting, is very clear. Stafford, Tripp, and Bienstock, p. 44.

24. See van Riel and van den Ban, in cooperation with Heijmans, p. 429.

25. Henderson *et al.*, p. 16.

26. Stafford, Tripp, and Bienstock, p. 38; Schechter, p. 36. This is, of course, an important result given that the most dominant logo is that of As-Sahab, al-Qaeda's media distribution wing, and its imitators, and that As-Sahab's logo is highly stylized script—which is to say, it falls far more to the "abstract" end of the spectrum. Of course, one of the most successful logos in the corporate world (and one of the most recognizable symbols in the world, period) is the Nike swoosh. But it is possible that there are some ways to make an abstract symbol more likely to work (Schechter, pp. 38-39), and it is still the case that *most* successful logos will not be abstract.

27. Henderson *et al.*, p. 24.

28. I am grateful to Michael P. Echemendia for this point.

29. See IntelCenter.

30. The clear preference for modern weapons is an interesting choice. While Hamas employs two crossed swords in their logo, almost all the Sunni groups, whether AQAM or Iraqi, choose modern weapons. According to the *Islamic Imagery Project*, p. 95, older weapons symbolize a linkage to ancient heroes, to earlier battles, the founders—which ideologically, one would assume would be a visual motif AQAM would be automatically drawn to. Modern weapons, on the other hand (p. 96):

> such as rifles and RPGs, illustrate the violent nature of ji-
> hadi warfare and also exaggerate the power of the jihadists'
> military technology. Modern weapons evoke modern jihadi
> victories (or perceived victories) such as the expulsion of the
> Soviets from Afghanistan. In this manner, modern weapons
> embody the inherent capacity of the jihadi movement to
> overcome and defeat the West, using the latter's own mili-
> tary technology. Modern weapons are also used by jihadi
> soldiers and martyrs to associate themselves with violent
> jihadi activism and construct their identities as participants
> in jihad.

31. IntelCenter.

32. *Ibid.*, p. 27.

33. Hamas has a pictogram of the al Aqsa mosque on its logo, but that is not particularly surprising, since it is a Pal-estinian group. Hezbollah, by contrast, has a globe. Iraq's Ji-hadist Leagues includes a map of Iraq; so do the Islamic Army in Iraq, the Islamic Movement for Mujahadeen, al Madinah al Muawarah Brigades. Neither is a particularly subtle visual argument.

34. *The Islamic Imagery Project,* p. 95. On the flag is the Muslim proclamation of faith.

35. The example of a successful abstract logo from the corporate world, of course, is the Nike "swoosh." Schechter, p. 38. Still, the fact that the logo incorporates a stylized letter may be why it is successful despite the fact that it is abstract and not representational (Schechter, p. 39):

> In situations where an abstract logo is clearly desirable—because a company is in a number of diverse fields, for example—it may be wise to consider integrating an initial letter into the design, so as to provide a 'memory peg' to new audiences, as Lexus has done. Of course, this would turn the abstract into a letter-symbol. If you use a pure abstraction, be prepared to support it more heavily than you might another type of logo.

In this case, the Arabic text reads simply "as Sahab," but the letters are separated, apparently for purely aesthetic reasons, whereas in the Arabic language letters are typically connected to one another, as would be the case in English cursive writing. To separate them in this fashion would only be done if the letters were here less intended as building blocks contributing to construction of a piece of text to be read, and more as individual aesthetic pieces to draw attention and be admired. There is a long history of Arabic calligraphy as an art form, linked to its development as the means through which the Qur'an—the received word of God—could be more widely transmitted and distributed. See David J. Roxburgh, *Writing the Word of God: Calligraphy and the Qur'an*, New Haven, CT: Yale University Press for the Houston Museum of Fine Arts, 2007; Abkelkebir Khatibi and Mohammed Kijelmassi, *The Splendor of Islamic Calligraphy*, New York: Thames and Hudson, Inc, 1994 Ed. Orig. *L'Art calligraphique de l'Islam* 1994, E. J. Emory, trans., 1194 Ed., Gallimard, Paris.

36. They are created using computer animation programs, and are not the work of actual animators. So the parallel in terms more familiar to a Western viewer would be the work of Pixar studios, where films are designed and executed using digital programs, not classic Warner Brothers or Walt Disney, where human artists physically drew cartoons one cell at a time.

37. That these high tech, professional graphics segments are being produced in Somalia is simply taken at face value by the overwhelming majority of commentators—certainly by the mainstream press outlets if they even bothered to cover the announcement of the *Network* at all. See, for example, Dana Hughes, "Somali Jihadis Launch 'News Channel' As Officials Warn of Growing Al Qaeda Links," ABC News, July 30, 2010, available from *abcnews. go.com/Blotter/al-shabab-somali-jihadis-launch-news-channel-officials/ story?id=11280279*. Only a minority of specialists pointed out the discrepancy between the state of the Somali countryside and the state of the media lab that would have been necessary to produce this graphics package. See Christopher Anzalone, "From 'Martyrdom' Videos to Jihadi Journalism in Somalia," *Informed Comment*, August 25, 2010:

> The rapid evolution of the group's multimedia productions raises questions of how and from where its media campaign is operated. . . the fast, high-level of improvement in production quality suggest that the group's multimedia network may include operatives based outside of war-torn Somalia in locations with ready access to high-speed Internet connections and multimedia design technology.

38. Gitte Lindgaard *et al*, "Attention Web Designers: You Have 50 Milliseconds to Make a Good First Impression," *Behaviour and Information Technology*, Vol. 25, No. 2, March/April 2006, pp. 115-126.

39. The best examples are the introductory graphics packages for the first video produced by the *Kataib News Network*, "Mogadishu: The Crusader's Graveyard," and Kavkaz Center Television, posted to YouTube under the title, "Kavkav Center Presents Footage of Mujahideen Routine Physical Training Mountains of Chechnya." The Kataib video's graphics are far more elaborate, so that, by comparison, the Kavkaz production actually looks cleaner and therefore more professional, but taken on their own, each is obviously based on a professional newscast. (Indeed, Kataib's graphics package lines up in perfect parallel with the introductory graphics packages of both *BBC International's World News*, and some of Al Jazeera's news programming.) It is far more than the best-trained individual could do, even with the most expensive computer and software—these graphics required a media lab to

produce. (The Kataib video survives on YouTube, but the original version, which was of far higher quality, has been taken down. Available from author upon request in .flv format.)

40. Kimmage and Rudlolfo, p. 44.

41. There may be ways to research the specific trajectories of AQAM logos: for example, are there shifts in the visual narratives associated with given logos over time? To an extent, can the target audiences be determined by where videos are released first (jihad-focused sites frequented only by those already converted versus more general use sites such as YouTube), or is the release timeline always the same? Are any changes to logos or shifts in animated shorts possible evidence that groups have reevaluated their media strategies, and, if so, is there any way to confirm that conclusion? (I am grateful to Michael P. Echemendia for this point.)

CHAPTER 7

CONCEPTUALIZING RADICALIZATION IN A MARKET FOR LOYALTIES

Shawn Powers
Matt Armstrong

The purpose of this chapter is to locate radicalization—the process of developing extremist ideologies and beliefs—in the broader context of strategic actors (e.g., states) competing for legitimacy in transnational public spheres. Radicalization is distinct from both terrorism and violent extremism, though it is often a precursor to the use of terrorist tactics and can be critical for creating broad support for extremist movements and behaviors.[1] Our primary concern here is not terrorism per se, but rather how strategic actors compete to radicalize communities against the established organs and apparatuses of a given society.

Borrowing from Monroe E. Price's 1994 model of the market for loyalties, we propose that radicalization and fascism represent two extremes on the same spectrum of citizen loyalty. Most governments encourage domestic citizenry to avoid either extreme, while at the same time engaging foreign citizens in ways that weaken their allegiances to their own governments. Emerging media technologies provide new structures for ideological transfer, enabling states and nonstate actors to compete for influence in a more balanced, transnational, ideational playing field. The stakes are significant, of course, with citizens clamoring for more transparent, fair, and efficacious governance, while increasingly threatening the legitimacy of states around the world.[2]

TECHNOLOGY AND RADICALIZATION

Communication technologies (including the Internet and text messaging) play a crucial role in the process of radicalization. These powerful platforms are particularly useful for those seeking to mobilize others disillusioned with the status quo that are similarly seeking out alternative fora where their perspectives may resonate with others. In cases of Islamic extremism, the message of violent jihad is more accessible and compelling to those who cannot read or speak Arabic through the dramatic growth of English websites, as well as those in other languages.[3] Anders Breivik, the Norwegian terrorist who killed 69 people in Oslo, Norway, in 2011, described his radicalization as an iterative process enabled by increasing involvement with a right-wing blog, "Gates of Vienna." Wade Michael Page, a neo-Nazi activist suspected of perpetrating the Gurdwara attack in Wisconsin in 2012, was closely affiliated with the online portal of the Hammerskin Nation, a skinhead movement operating across the United States. While typically categorized as "lone-wolf" or "school-shooter" incidents, the evidence suggests these violent extremists believed that they were representing a broader constituency. These constituencies are increasingly virtual, each built and maintained on the World Wide Web.[4]

This process of radicalization via digital information communication technologies (ICTs) benefits from an understanding of the broader context of how nation-states sustain shared identities and compete with other foreign actors to strengthen their own, while weakening others' standing among global citizens. Radicalization of a domestic group is of concern not simply because it represents a threat to the country's security, but also because it indicates that a citizen disregards a shared value and belief system from their home country for another. The ability to control domestic information flows has provided the nation-state its strength and stability since the Treaty of Westphalia in 1648. However, the declining cost to develop, send, and receive information across traditional barriers challenges states' capacities to control their domestic markets for ideas. For now, this weakening of information sovereignty permits greater competition over ideas between the citizenry and the state than had previously been possible. The current transition is best understood in the context of how emergent information technologies have historically created dynamic shifts in the constitution and legitimation of political power.

TECHNOLOGY, POWER, AND THE STATE

The production and dissemination of information is at the core of the modern Westphalian nation-state.[5] ICTs are an increasingly central element of 21st century statecraft, with adaptive political actors creating and controlling information flows in order to further their interests. At the same time, innovations in ICTs are typically couched in a discourse of furthering a universal right to free expression, often connected to a Kantian idea of coming closer to achieving a perpetual peace.[6] For example, at the turn of the 20th century, wireless telegraphy mastermind Guglielmo Marconi declared, "communication between peoples widely separated in space and thought is undoubtedly the greatest weapon against the evils of misunderstanding and jealousy."[7] The more connected the world is, the more difficult it is to engage in conflict, or so the thinking goes. Over a century later, U.S. Secretary of State Hillary Rodham Clinton echoed this sentiment, proposing a global right to connect to the World Wide Web: "Information freedom supports the peace and security that provides a foundation for global progress. Historically, asymmetrical access to information is one of the leading causes of interstate conflict."[8] A narrative of information as peace-inducing is firmly embedded within discourses of communication and technology. This narrative is, of course, strategic.

Appealing as the promise of information-driven peace may be, history offers ample evidence for skeptics. Not long after Marconi's radio was adopted by the Western world, German leaders deployed it as a tool of war, aiding Nazi aggression and Hitler's genocide of six million European Jews.[9] Just 6 months after Secretary Clinton spoke of the need for recognition of a universal right to connect to the World Wide Web, news broke that the U.S. Government, in coordination with its Israeli ally, deployed a cyber worm to slow Iran's nuclear program.[10] Despite theorization of an inevitable global village bound by transnational media flows and ubiquitous connectivity, states remain strategic actors, eager to adopt emerging technologies and adapt policy to advance national interests.[11]

Revolutions in communication technologies have had two, sometimes diametric, roles over the millennia. Francis Bacon first wrote, "*scientia potentia est,*" Latin for "knowledge is power." Indeed, enabling technologies capable of capturing and sharing information changes the constitution and sharing of knowledge (i.e., the collective belief in a set of truths) and thus, the constitution of power relations.[12] Analyzing the rise and fall of ancient Egyptian, Babylonian, Greek, and Roman Empires, Canadian historian Harold Innis found that every major communication technology contained intrinsic biases toward a particular organization and control of information, and thus shaped the constitution of authority.[13] For example, Latin script written on parchment, the medium of the Christian Church in the High and Late Middle Ages, created a monopoly of knowledge among the priests who were able to control access to the divine knowledge of the heavens. For the Church, its ability to have exclusive access to what society accepted as "divine knowledge" provided that body with the authority to prescribe social policy, holding sway over kings and citizens alike.

Benedict Anderson, Professor Emeritus at Cornell University, identified the adoption of the printing press in Europe as critical for the emergence of the modern nation-state. Arguing that no person could ever know every other member of her nation, Anderson's central research question was how nations—or, "imagined communities"—came to be. His research found that, as the printing press became more widespread in the 15th and 16th centuries, entrepreneurs began printing books and more transitory media in local vernaculars, rather than using the exclusive script languages, such as Latin, in order to maximize circulation and accessibility. This enabled rapid growth of local dialects and facilitated the emergence and codification of independent communities formed around a shared, common language. Documented, standardized, disseminated, and taught for generations, these shared discourses helped shape community values and norms. According to Anderson:

> The very possibility of imagining the nation only arose historically [with the emergence of] print-capitalism, which made it possible for rapidly growing numbers of people to think about themselves, and to relate themselves to others, in profoundly new ways. The first European nation-states were thus formed around their national print-languages.[14]

Historically, then, communication technologies have key roles to play in the development of organized communities.

The physical traits of a technology do not alone dictate particular communicative biases. Rather, the protocols and norms that govern how individuals share ideas and utilize technology dictate precisely how the technology will impact knowledge generation and legitimize (or de-legitimize) authority. For example, different alphabets—shared protocols for the exchange of ideas via text—necessarily have biases that permit or inhibit opportunities. Innis found that "a flexible alphabet favoured the growth of trade, development of the trading cities of the Phoenicians, and the emergence of smaller nations dependent on distinct languages."[15] The printing press itself did not cause a transition from tribes and empires to Westphalian sovereignty. Rather, the use of the printing press to produce locally authored books in indigenous languages fostered a shift in consciousness as to what constituted legitimate authority in Europe. Similarly, the Internet and the Global Positioning System (GPS), both products of the U.S. Defense Advanced Research Projects Agency (DARPA), facilitated and even encouraged the modern proliferation of social media, and the challenges they present for existing institutions. Emergent communication technologies facilitate change not simply through their existence, but through the specific socio-cultural and legal contexts that dictate how emerging media impress upon a society.

Just as the printing press reshaped the constitution of authority in the 16th century, in the 19th and early 20th century undersea cables and wireless telegraphy reshaped geopolitical power relations in the 20th century. Scholars have documented the role propaganda—"a one-way communication system designed to influence belief"—played in the conduct of 20th century foreign affairs, especially in times of conflict.[16] During World War I, allied forces severed German access to the world by cutting their cables. European news agencies friendly to their home government filtered and rewrote news sent abroad. In World War II, state-financed and operated international broadcasting was a critical tool of statecraft. Learning from their experiences of being isolated in World War I, the Nazis invested heavily in radio. It was so important to the Nazi's war efforts at home and abroad that they often targeted foreign radio transmitters first when invading a country. In turn, their own transmitters emerged as targets. According to Oigen Hadamowski, Director of Nazi Radio operations, "We spell radio with three exclamation marks because of its miraculous power—the strongest weapon ever given to the human spirit—that opens hearts and does not stop at borders."[17] Every government involved in World War II utilized propaganda to influence foreign opinions, with British broadcasting (e.g., the BBC Empire Service) holding particularly significant sway over European and American public opinions.[18] Arguably, British propaganda efforts were critical for propelling the United States to enter into both world wars.[19]

Modern advances in communication technologies are similarly reshaping power relations, but not necessarily in ways many predicted. *The New York Times* editorialist Thomas Friedman envisioned that, "the days when governments could isolate their people from understanding what life was like beyond their borders or even beyond their village are over."[20] Such optimistic, cyber-utopian predictions have been rampant, including among U.S. State Department diplomats.[21] Philip Taylor, former Chair of the Institute of Communications Studies at the University of Leeds, summed up such optimism when he wrote:

> Together with the internal combustion engine, penicillin and the splitting of the atom, [mass media] have served to transform the very nature not only of how human beings live their lives but of how they perceive the world around them.[22]

Yet, beneath Taylor's platitude is an argument with resonance: controlling information flows has become increasingly difficult, yet crucial, for state actors, and efforts at managing these flows are symbolic of the broader challenges that the modern era of globalization presents to state sovereignty, the defining building block of the modern international system. To explore how established and emerging international actors compete for ideational influence in the modern media ecology, we turn to a model of strategic international communication: Price's Market for Loyalties.[23]

RADICALIZATION IN THE MARKET FOR LOYALTIES

The market for loyalties model synthesizes propaganda, dialogue, and networked theories of strategic communication by suggesting that each approach is fundamentally driven by similar motivations and success or failure of the particularities of the ideational marketplace in question.[24] This market framework is grounded on a basic premise: International actors enact policies analogous to a strategic investment aiming to shape the allegiances of foreign audiences in ways that increase the likelihood of an outcome favored by the actor. In this marketplace, international actors (usually governments, but increasingly nonstate actors) are the sellers, and audiences are the buyers. Here, markets do not connect to modern capitalist or economic systems. This marketplace is not the same as the "free-market" ideology that is increasingly pervasive in political discourse. One need not agree with laissez-faire economic philosophy to appreciate a market as a system for determining mutually acceptable prices, or the terms of exchange between different actors. Market systems can assess, explain, and even predict human behavior in complex environments.[25] Thus, the market for loyalties is a means of conceptualizing how communication technologies, policies, and perceptions interact and shape the context within which radicalization, and its alternatives, occur.

At a rudimentary level, strategic actors are selling information in exchange for the audiences' attention, an increasingly scarce resource given the saturation of media markets around the world. Yet, actors are not simply selling information; rather, they are offering stories and identities that in some capacity reflect an ideological perspective. Audiences agree to "buy" what an actor is selling by repeatedly consuming and engaging with the ideational product, and in return, become increasingly loyal to the underlying narrative and its associated community.

Similar to any marketplace, the more an individual buys (in this case, consumes), the more they have to give (i.e., identify themselves with), and the more loyal they become to the investment's successful outcome and/or popularity. Thus, the more an audience tunes into an actor's media, the more they will identify with its messages and content. Consider support for partisan news media programming, (e.g., the editorial programming of *Al Jazeera* or *Fox News*) or the more subtle cultural or social messages embedded into the plots of cultural programs (e.g., *BBC World Service's* educational entertainment soap operas). This is not to say that media content inevitably "brain washes" viewing audiences. Rather, given the diversity and plethora of media options available today, audiences repeatedly tune into a particular network or YouTube channel because the outlets' programming resonates with or fulfills an ideational need.[26] More than ever, content is king. The medium is merely a component of the message.

Just as in commercial markets, the introduction of new competitors into an ideational market can have significant consequences for individuals and organizations. In Brazil, for example, the adoption of television in rural communities led to a more progressive climate for women's rights. Between 1970 and 1990, daily access to television in Brazil jumped from 10 to 80 percent. Popular *novelas* (soap operas) featuring strong, independent, educated, unmarried, and ambitious women provided compelling role models in rural areas where a woman's role was largely limited to childbearing and housework.[27] Access to television programming generally, and to *novelas* in particular, statistically correlated to substantial decreases in the birth rate, a key indicator of development and women's equality. Similar results occurred in India's rural communities when introduced to television (and local soap operas).[28]

In terms of the ideational marketplace, as a new communication technology (commercial satellites) decreased the cost of entering the market; a new seller (*Globo*, the producer of Brazil's *novelas*) provided a good (television programs) in high demand among buyers (Brazil's citizenry). The buyers compensated the seller through their loyalty to the programs, including discussing the programs with family and friends and consistently tuning in. Large, dedicated, and mobilized audiences are valuable to advertisers and, in return, generate substantial revenue for the seller.

The introduction of a new competitor, in this case, altered the marketplace of loyalties through enhanced competition, eventually resulting in changes in consumer behaviors. Policymakers should take note that the introduction of a new competitor itself is not necessarily transformational. Rather, the new competitor's ability to identify and react to unmet demand shifted loyalties and eventually consumers' habits.

The entrance of new competitors, especially in imperfect or distorted markets, can also be highly disruptive. In Sinjar, a tradition-bound community in Northwest Iraq, exposure to media reflecting Western values contributed to increased suicides among teenage women. Between 2011 and June 2012, 50 teenage girls killed themselves, either through self-immolation or gunshot.[29] While not only a staggering number of suicides for Iraqis, it is among the top five worst per capita female teenage suicide rates in the world. Interviews with girls who survived the suicide attempts indicate that access to the Internet and satellite TV were crucial in exposing girls to "glimpses of a better life, unencumbered by the traditions that have constricted women for centuries."[30] Locals blame the widely popular Turkish soap opera, *Forbidden Love*, for raising expectations among teenage Iraqis of a life defined not by obedience and child rearing, but rather of individualism and romance. According to Iraqi journalist Kheri Shingli, "The girls feel they are not living their life well compared to the rest of the world."[31] Just as the introduction of new technology-driven platforms often radically disrupt existing business models in a static market (e.g., Craigslist's impact on the newspaper industry, and Wikipedia's impact on *Encyclopedia Britannica*), dramatic change in a closed ideational marketplace can have unexpected, detrimental consequences as well. (See Figure 7-1.)

		Commerce	Ideas
Buyers	Who:	Individuals, businesses	Citizens, subjects, nationals, and consumers
	What:	Currency, barter	Attention, identity, loyalty, agency
	Why:	Basic needs, shared identity	Connect with others, make sense of lived experience
Sellers	Who:	Producers, distributors (i.e. cartels)	Governments, businesses, interest groups (i.e. cartels)
	What:	Goods and Services	Information, propaganda, news and entertainment
	Why:	Meet needs, further cartel interests	Meet needs, further cartel interests

Figure 7-1. Comparing Commerce and Idea-Based Markets.

We propose using the market for loyalties as a means for state actors to conceptualize how communication technologies and policy interact and shape the context within which radicalization occurs. Here, radicalization is one extreme, whereby a citizen defects (either ideologically, physically, or both) from his or her home country, pledging allegiance to another political actor whose interests are necessarily at odds with the home country's interests. On the other end of the extreme is fascism, an authoritarian nationalist political ideology whereby a citizen pledges loyalty to the state regardless of its legitimacy or capacity to govern. Most states operate in between the two extremes, careful not to encourage a fascist ideology at home, nor pursue radicalization of foreign citizens. The rationale is fairly simple: fascist political regimes limit a government's capacity to maneuver successfully the changing contours of a globalized geopolitics, while radicalizing foreign populations similarly risks long-term threats to state-survival (e.g., radicalizing the Mujahideen ultimately makes working with its modern incarnate, the Taliban, extraordinarily difficult). The majority of citizens remain in between fascism and radicalization with states and political actors using technology and policy to compete for their loyalties.

Sellers.

Why do international actors invest in the market for loyalties? One clear winner from the current processes of globalization has been the citizen. Governments around the world are facing increasingly activated, mobilized, and intelligent citizen groups calling for government reform and accountability. The Arab

Spring demonstrated how powerful these movements are in bringing about dramatic change — even regime change — in just a matter of weeks.[32]

The U.S. Government invests in the marketplace of loyalties through its international broadcasting to improve the likely acceptance of its foreign policies and national interests (e.g., democracy in the Middle East) and/or to increase interest in its private sector goods and services (e.g., increased acceptance of Coca-Cola products and Facebook's web services). Similar to the plethora of rationales one relies upon when investing in a stock market (e.g., financial profit, ideological support for the corporation's mission, the possibility of undercutting a competitor by investing in its partners, etc.), the precise reasons for any actor's intervention into another's information space vary significantly and over time.

As foreign actors appeal to a country's domestic audiences through communication technologies, governments are eager to restrict access to content that could impact negatively a citizen's loyalty to his regime. They also provide more appealing information (propaganda), favorable economic policy, and robust social services to court domestic constituencies. In January 2011, for example, former Egyptian President Hosni Mubarak ordered a shutdown of all Internet services in an effort to regain control over the flow of information during protests that eventually would force his removal from power. President Mubarak implemented this draconian measure only after weeks of revved-up government propaganda disseminated via terrestrial television and radio services. China, too, is keen to protect its information space from foreign interventions, deploying a mix of censorship, propaganda, and market solutions to increase the amount of web content that strengthens shared Chinese nationalism and shared values.

As economic interests increasingly become interconnected with a state's national interests, governments are moving to regulate international information flows in ways that preserve their national economic advantage. In the United States, for example, growing political interest exists in expanding the monitoring and regulation of Internet traffic not for the purpose of political censorship, but rather to enhance the security of web services (e.g., Google, Facebook, and eTrade) and protect intellectual property (e.g., music, movies, and television programming) that drive the nation's economic growth.[33] While the motivations and tactics Egypt, China, and the United States use are quite diverse, analytically speaking, they are similar in the sense that they represent government efforts to shape the marketplace of information flows for the purpose of national survival.

Loyalty to a state is not merely an abstract idea either. With transnational flows of goods, services, and information as the norm, citizens increasingly are able to identify with and support states that best protect their interests. Facebook co-founder Eduardo Saverin's high-profile renunciation of U.S. citizenship, opting instead for Singapore citizenship, is an illustrative case of acting in one's own self-interest. According to Saverin's attorney, "U.S. citizens are severely restricted as to what they can invest in and where they can maintain accounts. Many foreign funds and banks won't accept Americans." Having lived in Singapore since 2009, Saverin feels that the city-state is "an attractive place to live and a convenient travel hub for doing business in Asia."[34] In this case, loyalty to Singapore was seen as best protecting Saverin's economic interests, reflecting a prioritization of laissez-faire market values and concerns of undue restrictions on the citizenry (e.g., sanctions against trade with Iran). Saverin is not simply an outlier. The number of Americans relinquishing their citizenship increased from 226 to 1,780 between 2008 and 2011, which is to say, an American is 688 times more likely to self-denaturalize in 2011 than in 2008. Saverin reflects a trend among the elite, who are able to shift their citizenship as a result of a more appealing set of policies and/or ideological affiliations.[35] In some of these cases, radicalization comes in the form of free-market fundamentalism, where a citizen is more trusting of a laissez-faire market system than to a state perceived as misallocating its tax revenues (e.g., Universal Health Care) or placing undue restrictions on private citizen behavior (e.g., restricting trade with Iran).

Buyers.

Why do citizens engage in the market for loyalties? Human nature includes an innate fear of social isolation and, early on, we demonstrate the need for acceptance into something greater than the individual self: a community.[36] Before the existence of mass media, children were born into a family that would serve as an immediate community and gradually introduced other elements of their collective communities—friends, aunts and uncles, colleagues, and so on.[37] Today, mass media, and increasingly social media, play an important psychosocial role in establishing community, or put another way, establishing shared knowledge, norms, and interests.

Ulrich Beck argues that one consequence of the rapid globalization witnessed in the past 25 years is the shattering of the traditional means of community formation and maintenance, both in relation to the hyper local (e.g., the family) and the societal (e.g., the nation).[38] Similar to how a family introduced itself to the local community, the nation-state, on a larger scale, was the primary means through which citizens engaged the international community. This, of course, is changing, given the nature of modern communications networks. Before commercial satellites, 99 percent of communication occurred within the boundaries of the nation-state.[39] Anderson's conception of the nation as an "imagined community" worked because diverse groups shared nation-based media that constituted shared histories, stories, and knowledge. As information flows become more difficult to control at the level of the state, and as communication technologies become more mobile, affordable, and globally connected, people began to form their own imagined communities, not based on established authority and tradition, but rather on their personal interests, ideas, and passions. Globally connected media offer a more robust market for news, information, and entertainment, each of which, in turn, shape the modern citizen's loyalties and sense of citizenship.

What do radicals have in common with people only modestly shifting their allegiances? Radicalization is an extreme, whereby a citizen necessarily defects from her home country, pledging allegiance to an alternative strategic actor and its ideological worldviews. Short of radicalization, foreign information flows influence citizens with the potential to shift loyalties from one strategic actor to another. While radicalization represents one end of the spectrum, less severe defections can also have consequences for a state's security. From the perspective of the state, new information flows not only risk full-scale defections (e.g., radicalization), but also minor defections, whereby citizens split their loyalties between several actors, or simply become less and less concerned with their home state. As citizens become less eager to back a state's policies, tax revenues are likely to decrease, and support for war efforts may quickly fall. If a state becomes desperate and, as a result, resorts to violence to ensure citizen compliance with state regulations, its citizens may challenge the government's legitimacy among domestic and international actors. Tunisia, Egypt, and Syria each present compelling anecdotes of how quickly a state's legitimacy and prospects for survival can fall. Even if President Bashar al-Assad is able to survive, events on the ground will weaken Syria for years to come, thereby making it less able to compete economically and militarily. Not only is the Arab Spring a stark reminder for how quickly citizens can threaten a regime's survival in draconian conditions, but it also demonstrates how foreign information flows act as critical variables in shaping the modern citizen's loyalties.

IMPLICATIONS

Two theoretical approaches, thus far, have dominated international communications research addressing the question of radicalization: propaganda and dialogue. Yet, when examined using contemporary, empirical analysis, each has flaws. For example, given the growing complexity of information sources, the propaganda approach as a prescriptive one is woefully outmoded. Audiences can too easily dismiss foreign information campaigns that fail to satisfy their increasingly potent ability to fulfill their media preferences. Alternatively, propositions for "dialogue" in public diplomacy outline a dialogic disposition, which involves two-way communication, listening as well as speaking, calling for a constructive, ethically-grounded intervention into a foreign public sphere.[40] Yet this model is rife with political impracticalities. Increasingly media-savvy publics will be skeptical of promises of dialogue, which require genuine (non-strategic) listening and a willingness to change policies on behalf of state actors.[41] States are not likely to change their policies based upon the opinions of foreign populations, because governments are not accountable to them in any direct or institutional way. It is improbable that any government will listen to the degree promised by the term dialogue.

Viewing radicalization as part of the broader spectrum of possibilities in a market for loyalties is helpful for practitioners in a number of ways. First, radicalization operates within the confines of a state-based international system, whereby radical values or actions compare to the shared values and behaviors of a nation-state. Radical attitudes and behaviors in one context may not be radical in another, and nation-states remain the primary building blocks of the international system. The relative significance of nonstate actors is measured vis-à-vis their threat to a nation-state or states, and their ultimate goal is typically some form of state-status and/or sovereignty.

This does not leave the concept of radicalization devoid of value; rather, it suggests the parameters of radicalization research. Such parameters are productive in providing clarity in defining the terms and scope of the required policy mechanisms. Combating global radicalization from a conceptual level is extraordinarily challenging as every country defines radicalization vis-à-vis local customs and values. Combating radicalization at the domestic level is possible and is something that every government already does through the regulation and manipulation of its information ecology, in addition to using traditional law enforcement tools. Radicalization and fascism are two extremes sitting along the same spectrum of loyalties.

Locating radicalization as a state-based concept is instructive for foreign policy, too. Actors interested in destabilizing foreign countries use information interventions to compete for citizen attention and loyalty, thus weakening foreign governments. America's commitment to a right to free expression, even of extraordinarily hostile speech functions as an extremist belief to the governments of China and Iran, for example. Freedom of expression is a central part of "21st Century Statecraft," according to Secretary Clinton.[42] As the global competition for power creasingly is inintertwined with ideological battles over how society should be structured and governments compete to defend and extend their ideological interests, global information flows and interventions inherently may be seen as potentially radicalizing. This includes English-language jihadist chat rooms, but also the efforts to establish a universal right to connect freely to the Internet. Thus, this "soft" side of power, typically seen as a subsidiary to the use of force, is increasingly capable of engendering hard-power responses. Osama bin Laden's al-Qaeda, for example, was as much a reaction to Western cultural influence as the presence of American troops in Muslim-majority countries. Given the existence of, and continued interest in, expanding constraints on the use of force against other states, communication technology tools of soft influence, operating with fewer legal constraints while shaping the markets for loyalties, could easily become the central arena for geopolitical competition in the years to follow.

Second, historically, emerging communication technologies reshape how societies negotiate power and legitimate authority. From the creation of the alphabet to the printing press, technologies that enable new forms of expression necessarily force established political institutions to adapt or die. Each technology has specific biases that benefit particular actors. As societies moved from spoken to written word, for example, orators had to compete for authority that previously illiterate populations bestowed. Digital information technologies need to be understood in this historical context. They have specific biases that are different from analogue and interpersonal communication, and actors that are best able to adapt to the tactics of digital communication will be the ones best suited to lead in the 21st century. While a discussion of the specific biases of digital communications technologies is outside the scope of this chapter, governance and policy require rethinking in the modern Information Age. Forward thinking policymakers should understand how major information technologies impact power relations in national and international contexts, and apply this analysis to policies aiming to help states establish and maintain legitimacy with domestic and foreign audiences. Moreover, once analyzed through the market model, the maintenance and manipulation of loyalties could be guided by empirically grounded micro-economic principles, including: supply and demand; perfect competition; market failure; resource allocation; optimal welfare; opportunity cost; transaction costs; information asymmetry; signaling;

behavioral economics; and saturated, latent, ignored, missing and lost markets.[43]

Third, the market for loyalties provides a model for understanding the different ways actors compete for influence, including efforts at radicalizing foreign citizens. The market analogy identifies state and non-state actors and citizens as strategic entities, buying and selling goods and services, driven by perceived needs and desires. It also provides a rubric for understanding the different means by which states can defend against radicalization, at each of the levels of policy, communication, technology, and infrastructure. For example, in response to a growing threat of homegrown radicalization, a state could utilize new technologies to connect with or monitor its estranged citizens, enact policies incentivizing nationalism and de-radicalization, launch a robust counter-radicalization information campaign targeting the most vulnerable populations, and/or alter the communication infrastructure by levying hefty taxes on Internet data coming from or being sent abroad.

Similar to how Henry Ford's commercial car disrupted the market for horses early in the 20th century, digital information technologies, and the Internet in particular, have opened up the market for loyalties in transformative ways. But the 21st century will not be nearly as chaotic, or deviate from traditional geopolitics as many digital evangelists would like to believe. States adjust. Demands for governance will grow. Chaos breeds structure and stability. The market for loyalties provides policymakers a model for understanding all of the different pieces of the puzzle that may otherwise seem like an uncontrollable, unmanageable global grab for power. States compete for power and influence in an international market of loyalties. Other actors compete, though typically not at the same level as states as they lack the policy tools and resources governments are able to wield. States are engaging in an ideological conflict over the restructuring of societies. Actors create new information flows and the infrastructure that enables the dissemination of new information flows to strengthen their capacity to compete in the marketplace. Similar to commercial markets, they team up and form cartels, strengthening their place in the market vis-à-vis competitors. The strongest states will be those able to identify the specific material and ideational needs of target populations and create structures, policies, and programs to sustain citizen loyalties, both at home and abroad.

ENDNOTES - CHAPTER 7

1. For more on the distinction of these terms, see Chapter 2.

2. Manuel Castells, *Communication Power*, New York: Oxford University Press, 2011.

3. Donna Abu-Nasr and Lee Keath, "200 Websites Spread Al-Qaida's Message in English: Increasing Numbers of Radical Islamic Websites Are Spreading al-Qaida's Message in English," *The Associated Press*, November 14, 2009.

4. Jamie Bartlett, Jonathan Birdwell, and Mark Littler, *The New Face of Digital Populism*, London, UK: Demos, 2011.

5. Benedict Anderson, *Imagined Communities: Reflections on the Origin and Spread of Nationalism*, New York: Verso, 1983; Sandra Braman, *Change of State: Information, Policy, and Power*, Cambridge, MA: MIT Press, 2007.

6. Immanuel Kant, *Perpetual Peace, and Other Essays on Politics, History, and Morals*, Ted Humphrey, trans., Indianapolis, IN: Hackett Pub Co., 1795 (1983).

7. Guglielmo Marconi, "Broadcast to the United States of America," BBC, November 27, 1923, available from *markpadfield.com/marconicalling/museum/html/objects/ephemera/objects-i=841.005-t=2-n=0.html.*

8. Hillary Rodham Clinton, "Remarks on Internet Freedom," Washington, DC: U.S. Department of State, January 21, 2010, available from *www.state.gov/secretary/rm/2010/01/135519.htm.*

9. Martin Doherty, *Nazi Wireless Propaganda: Lord Haw-Haw and British Public Opinion*, Edinburgh, Scotland: Polygon, 2000.

10. David Sanger, *Confront and Conceal: Obama's Secret Wars and Surprising Use of American Power*, New York: Crown, 2012.

11. Jean-Marie Guehenno, *End of the Nation-State*, Minneapolis, MN: University of Minnesota Press, 2000; Michael Hardt and Antonio Negri, *Empire*, Cambridge, MA: Harvard University Press, 2001; Kenichi Ohmae, *The End of the Nation State: The Rise of Regional Economies*, New York: Free Press, 1996; Manuel Castells, *The Rise of the Network Society*, Malden, MA: Blackwell Publishers, 1996.

12. Michel Foucault, *Knowledge/power: Selected Readings: Selected Interviews and Other Writings, 1972-77*, New York: Pantheon Books, 1980.

13. Harold Innis, *The Bias of Communication*, Toronto, Ontario, Canada: University of Toronto Press, 1951; Harold Innis, *Empire and Communication*, Toronto, Ontario, Canada: University of Toronto Press, 1950.

14. Anderson, p. 36.

15. Innis, *Empire and Communication*, p. 39.

16. James Wood, *The History of International Broadcasting*, London, UK: The Institution for Engineering and Technology, 1992, p. 25.

17. Cited by Julian Hale, *Radio Power: Propaganda and International Broadcasting*, Philadelphia, PA: Temple University Press, 1975, p. 1.

18. Philip M. Taylor, *Munitions of the Mind*, Manchester, UK: Manchester University Press, 2003.

19. Nicholas J. Cull, *The Cold War and the United States Information Agency*, Cambridge, MA: Cambridge University Press, 2008.

20. Thomas Friedman, *The Nexus and the Olive Tree: Understanding Globalization*, Harpswell, ME: Anchor, 2000, p. 66.

21. Jesse Lichtenstein, "Digital Diplomacy," *New York Times Magazine*, July 16, 2010.

22. Philip Taylor, *Global Communications, International Affairs and the Media Since 1945*, London, UK: Routledge, 1997, p. 24.

23. Monroe E. Price: "The Market for Loyalties: Electronic Media and the Global Competition for Allegiances," *The Yale Law Journal*, Vol. 104, No. 3, December 1, 1994, pp. 667-705.

24. Jacques Ellul, *Propaganda: The Formation of Men's Attitudes*, London, UK: Vintage, 1973; Shaun Riordan, *Dialogue-based Public Diplomacy: A New Foreign Policy Paradigm*, No. 95, The Hague, The Netherlands: Netherlands Institute for International Relations, 2004.

25. Tim Harford, *The Undercover Economist*, Oxford, UK: Oxford University Press, 2005; Mariano Tommasi and Kathryn Ierull, *The New Economics of Human Behaviour*, Cambridge, MA: Cambridge University Press, 1995.

26. Sandra J. Ball-Rokeach, "The Origins of Individual Media-System Dependency," *Communication Research*, Vol. 12, No. 4, October 1, 1985, pp. 485-510.

27. Eliana La Ferrara, Alberto Chong, and Suzanne Duryea: "Soap Operas and Fertility: Evidence from Brazil," *Working Paper*, No. 172, Cambridge, MA: Bureau for Research and Economic Analysis of Development, March 2008.

28. Robert Jensen and Emily Oster, "The Power of TV: Cable Television and Women's Status in India," *The Quarterly Journal of Economics*, Vol. 124, No. 3, 2009, pp. 1057-1094.

29. Some dispute the actual cause of death. There is evidence that, in some cases, teenage girls were killed as so-called honor killings, a ritual that allows for the brutal punishment of Muslim women seen as disobeying family and/or religion. See "Honour killings: Plague of Suicides in North May Actually Be Murder," *Niqash*, October 1, 2012, available from *www.niqash.org/articles/print.php?id=2968&lang=en.*

30. Tim Arango, "Where Arranged Marriages Are Customary, Suicides Grow More Common," *The New York Times*, June 7, 2012, p. A12.

31. *Ibid.*

32. Haley Edwards, "Former Al Jazeera Head on Quitting, the Arab Spring, and Qatar's Role," *The Atlantic*, September 30, 2011, available from *www.theatlantic.com/international/archive/2011/09/former-al-jazeera-head-on-quitting-the-arab-spring-and-qatars-role/245932/.*

33. "Intellectual Property and the U.S. Economy: Industries in Focus," Washington, DC: U.S. Department of Commerce, April 10, 2012, available from *www.esa.doc.gov/Reports/intellectual-property-and-us-economy-industries-focus.*

34. Shibani Mahtani, "Asia's Lighter Taxes Provide a Lure," *The Wall Street Journal*, May 17, 2012, p. C3.

35. *Ibid.*

36. Elisabeth Noelle Neumann: "The Spiral of Silence A Theory of Public Opinion," *Journal of Communication,* Vol. 24, No. 2, June 1, 1974, pp. 43-51.

37. *Ibid.*

38. Ulrich Beck, *Power in the Global Age: A New Global Political Economy*, Cambridge, MA: Polity Press, 2005.

39. Joseph N. Pelton and Robert J. Oslund, *Communications Satellites: Global Change Agents*, New York: Psychology Press, 2004, p. 27.

40. William P. Kiehl, *America's Dialogue with the World*, Washington, DC: Public Diplomacy Council, 2006; Marc Lynch, "The Dialogue of Civilizations and International Public Spheres," *Millennium: Journal of International Studies,* Vol. 29, No. 20, 2000, pp. 307-330; Marc Lynch, "Transnational Dialogue in an Age of Terror," *Global Society,* Vol. 19, No. 1, 2005, pp. 5-28; Peter G. Peterson, "Public Diplomacy and the War on Terrorism," *Foreign Affairs* Vol. 81, No. 5, 2002, pp. 74-94; Olivier Zöllner, "A Quest for Dialogue in International Broadcasting: Germany's Public Diplomacy Targeting Arab Audiences," *Global Media and Communication,* Vol. 2, No. 2, 2006, pp. 160-182.

41. Shaun Riordan: "Dialogue-Based Public Diplomacy: A New Foreign Policy Paradigm?" *Discussion Papers in Diplomacy*, No. 95, 2004, p. 8.

42. Clinton.

43. For more on the application of micro-economic principles to competitions for citizen loyalty between state and nonstate actors, see Shawn Powers: "Microeconomic Theory & Strategic Communication: Advancing a Market for Loyalties Model of Public Diplomacy," International Communication Association Annual Conference, London, UK, June 2013.

CHAPTER 8

SEMANTIC PROCESSING OF VISUAL PROPAGANDA IN THE ONLINE ENVIRONMENT

Saeid Balkesim

During periods of peace and war, images have served as important propaganda tools for many centuries. The recent influx of multimedia information distributed over the World Wide Web, however, adds exponentially to the corpus of such activities. The Dark Web research team from the University of Arizona, Tempe, AZ, identifies close to half a billion postings from 10,000 websites that contain extremist or terrorist material.[1] The availability of social media as a distribution platform further inflates the size of searchable content. The estimated number of images on Facebook alone is 100 billion.[2] The already extensive, expanding volume of visual messaging in the online environment heightens the complexity of tracking extremists' use of propaganda.

Designing a robust, content-based image retrieval system is even more of a challenge because of extremists' recurrent use of image manipulation to influence viewers' opinions.[3] Many factors have facilitated their ability to manipulate images readily, including the availability of image/video editing software bundled freely with other products, the availability of such products easily downloadable from the Internet, the abundance of online video post-production tutorials, and the wide range of affordable high quality image capturing devices such as scanners and cameras. With access to such tools, extremists can capture any publicly available image, manipulate it, and reproduce it to serve the message strategy of their propaganda efforts. By removing particular components of images and inserting replacement components, extremists can often avoid detection by standard image retrieval systems.[4]

Thus, studying the impact of digitally manipulated images is essential to finding effective means of countering these messages and minimizing any damaging effects they have. This kind of analysis, however, requires accurate detection and isolation of such altered images. Here, I will offer the means of developing a semantic visual propaganda database to achieve that goal. The semantic approach offers a seamless way to accommodate several semantic or meaning-based rules that interdisciplinary experts studying transcultural violence can modify to control the system's performance. Further, the semantic system offers a direct way of developing adequate computational tools capable of detecting a digital image that has been modified to appear visually different from the original.[5]

To explain the semantic approach and its potential to assist in the efficient retrieval of extremists' use of visual propaganda, I will begin by presenting an overview of the main problems with current image retrieval systems. I will then explain the main components of the semantic database and offer "best practices" analytical approaches for using the system. I will conclude by outlining the benefits of using the semantic database approach.

PROBLEMS WITH CURRENT IMAGE RETRIEVAL AND CATALOGING SYSTEMS

Current techniques that track and locate sources of images and videos posted by violence promoters rely on a set of assumptions about images and/or videos that prevent retrieval of many items needed for comprehensive analyses. In short, current image search techniques rely on *syntactic image retrieval systems*. The syntactic retrieval approach is very similar to the traditional search for key words in a document. The syntax that generates a sentence matches its closest resemblance in a database word by word and in a grammatically defined order. The application of the syntactical approach in the case of altered images, however, is less than ideal due to the fact that the contents of the original image that analysts are searching for are no longer the same.

A major problem of the syntactic retrieval approach is its reliance on sequentially matching all symbols that represent a particular, static image. These symbols appear in lexical order in the database. Lexically ordered items follow alphabetical order similar to word entries in linguistic dictionaries. While a fast and accurate method for matching single items, search engines designed and built to follow this lexical order are very rigid; they do not allow retrieval based on the arbitrary relationships between items. For example, if we are syntactically searching for an image that the database represents symbolically with a square on top, followed by a disc in the middle and a star at the bottom, the search would fail if no image satisfies that order, even if images included in the database contain all three items.

The same difficulties with a lexical ordering approach also apply to videos since, as they become a part of databases, videos convert into "key image frames." A sequence of image frames makes up each video. Each image frame is a single, static image that contains information in every pixel within the space of each frame, generally referred to as spatial information. Conventionally, those retrieving video frames use syntactic approaches despite the fact that the frames represent another example of sequentially ordered items, which as previously noted, causes problems for any comprehensive retrieval of extremist groups' distribution of images.

Proposing a change from an exclusive reliance on syntactical systems of image retrieval may be a concern to some, based on fears that the move might compromise the efficient processing capabilities that now characterize syntactic systems. Such worries, however, are unnecessary. The majority of the frames in videos do, in fact, contain redundant information and very few frames contain new and essential information. The video summarization techniques I propose as replacements are very useful in filtering out the redundant frames, leaving only the key frames to deal with in a smaller video clip. The summarized video represented in key image frames therefore is more ideal for our suggested database than the entirety of the original video.

Most video summarization techniques use spatial domain information to cluster image frames into several levels of relevance. The video summarizer uses image frames to produce image clusters using one of the popular clustering techniques, such as the k-means algorithm, to cluster several video clips into video segments. For example, if there are three main colors within a certain video clip, the k-means calculates the mean value of each color, and arranges all video frames in terms of their relevance to these colors. Analysts use the similarity and dissimilarity of frames relative to those colors in each video segment using any of the known distance measures.[6] The main benefit of spatial video summarization is that it produces a collection of relevant frames with respect to certain spatial activities within a video clip and eliminates frames redundant to the same activities.

DESCRIPTION OF THE SEMANTIC DATABASE

Semantic databases offer a needed revision to syntactic systems of image retrieval. The semantic database organizes images based on relationships extracted from semantic rules. Users of the database set the initial rules to serve their specific requirements and they can add more rules and relations to reorganize the content of the database to fit their own requirements. The preset semantic rules function to categorize the images in the database. As the database expands in size, the system adapts to the newly added images by placing them within their proper semantic locations. Semantic databases expose relationships between various visual components within the same category or between different categories.[7] As the database grows, the relationships between the elements strengthen. The creation of seamless combinations of semantically connected objects within the same database requires the integration of several tools that serve a unified purpose of accurate representation of the actual data. Below, I will describe six of the major highlights of the semantic approach: image segmentation, keyword bags, multimedia posting conversion, image component labels, video summarization, and self-correcting semantic features.

Image Segmentation.

The most effective way to describe an image semantically is to segment it into its constitutive parts. The more descriptions assigned to the image components, the richer the semantic image database. The diagram in Figure 8-1 shows an example of a semantic segmentation approach utilizing five ways to subdivide an image: color, object size, object density, object mixture, and object shape features. The varying contributions of each of the five parameters form the final outcome of the segmented object, which function as the semantic rules.

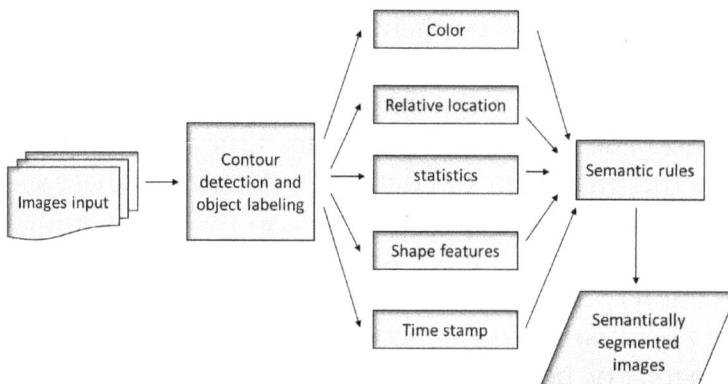

Figure 8-1. Semantic Image Segmentation Flow Chart.

A standard shape library stores and categorizes the basic shapes generated by semantic segmentation. This library functions to match any new or unknown object with the one that already exists in the library.

Image segmentation is one of critical parts necessary to accomplish the best shape interpretation and achieve successful pattern recognition. Generally, the classical segmentation algorithms use sharp changes in pixel intensity values to partition an image into regions. The semantic segmentation combines with the classical approach as a preprocessing stage for contour detection and object labeling as shown in Figure 8-1.

The object retrieval and matching stage combines the results of several algorithms using a procedure known as "decision fusion" to improve retrieval outcomes beyond those obtainable from any of the individual methods alone. The same procedure can be used to combine the five segmentation algorithms in the above example to generate a semantic image segmentation system, based on rules fine-tuned by the opinions of experts or the results of experiments of target audience members.

Keyword Bags.

The semantic shape segmentation groups encompass local image regions or textures that share common shape features together to form one cluster. Several shape descriptors combine to achieve the task of detecting these local shape features. The lowest three moment orders, for example, represent the shape area, centroid (the middle point of the shape) and variance respectively. More features of a particular shape add on as the moment orders increase. A large library of these features can form a dictionary in which each cluster functions as a word that represents a particular visual pattern. Using this process of semantic word collection, a bag of visual pattern words can describe an image.[8] An example of this would be two shapes that share similar color and appear next to each other in a particular orientation. The collection of visual pattern words is analogous to the bag-of-words representation used in natural language and text-document processing. This analogy facilitates borrowing techniques developed for natural language processing into image processing.

Multimedia Posting Conversions.

The conversion of multimedia web postings to a semantic database is a key component of the construction of the semantic database. The online postings may include text, audio, video, and images in many combinations. For the purpose of consistency and ease of processing in the semantic database approach, the proposed system should convert the video to key frames using video summarization techniques and transform audio into text using speech-processing techniques. The final outcome of the multimedia file would therefore be images and text. The conversion of text into text summaries using text summarization techniques reduces the burden on the semantic processing of text data. The key images produced by the video summarizer are semantically segmented into components that fit with the earlier definition of the semantic framework. Each video frame constitutes several segmented objects that may share similar features with objects in other frames. Therefore, the semantic rule criteria can be extended to cover several frames.

Image Component Labels.

The segmentation of 2D images into smaller image objects that represent the basic components contained in each single frame is essential for the semantic shape retrieval. The ideal method is to use a tree-mapped data structure based on object contours. Contour pixels are the outlying points that enclose an object in a particular 2D image. The semantic system maps the whole image data set into the hierarchical tree structure used in the establishment of an extensible markup language (xml) database for each image. A preprocessing stage that involves image enhancement, optimal thresholding, edge detection, and object contour segmentation is essential to the success of the whole system. (See Figure 8-2.)

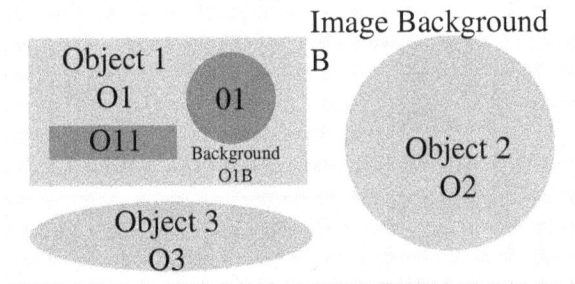

Figure 8-2. Sequential Contour Assignment.

Standard edge detection algorithms suffer from the lack of continuity of edges, thereby requiring a post-processor to link the broken edges.[9] The linking algorithms may introduce unnecessary ambiguity and incorrect links of "noisy" data. To overcome this problem, Saeid Belkasim, Xiangu Hong, and Otman

Badir used an automatic segmentation method based on an optimum automatic thresholding procedure combined with an edge detector.[10] This approach produced a continuously connected object border suitable for the hierarchical object tree structure and leads to a fully segmented image. Figure 8-3 shows an example of constructing the hierarchical tree data structure.

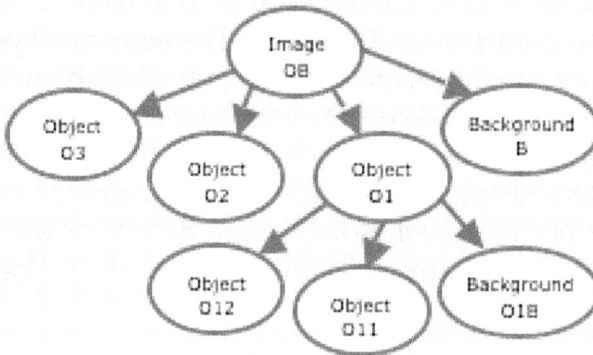

Figure 8-3. The Hierarchical Tree Data Structure.

The produced xml semantic database, built for each segmented object, functions for object retrieval and analysis, as each segmented image object boundary (contour) is the basic retrieval guide in the database. Figure 8-4 summarizes the above steps of image labeling.

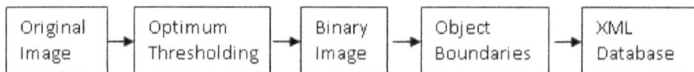

Figure 8-4. Generation of Object XML Database.

Video Summarization.

A video consists of a large number of image frames. The majority of these frames contain similar scenes, and only a few key frames contain new visual information. Video summarization is the process of removing all redundant image frames and retaining a few key image frames. These key images can be processed as individual images to be used in our database as shown in Figure 8-4. The key frames produced are usually enough to give an indication of the content of the video since the summarizers filter out similar frames and leave only dissimilar frames. Users can measure the similarity and dissimilarity of frames in each video segment using any of the known distance measures such as the Euclidean distance.[11] The summarization allows the feature extraction stage to save a considerable amount of computation time by dealing with just a few frames instead of the whole video.

Self-Correcting Semantic Features.

The semantic retrieval system can build in semantic verification the same way grammar and semantic rules work in natural language. In some cases, a group of words may be grammatically correct, but simultaneously semantically incorrect and vice versa, for example "a man is younger than his son." Objects embedded in images function in similar ways. Two objects that never appear together naturally in one image can violate one of the database's natural existence rules. For example, a light source pointed in one direction contradicts the direction of the shadow in the same scene.

SEMANTIC PATTERN DISCOVERY
AND ANALYSIS

Pattern analysis makes use of the availability of semantic data from the semantic database utilizing several statistical pattern analysis tools. Comparing unknown images to a library of known prototypes and extracting statistical information about the unknown images is an example of such tools. Another example would be to form a set of visual communication rules and use them to refine the results of the pattern analysis stage. Other forms of data available from a semantic database would be the date and time of an image's creation. Such information may also be used in the formation of the semantic rules and can narrow the pool of candidate images for analysis. In an attempt to prove that a doctored image is not credible, for example, analysts could retrieve its original copy and use it as a basis of comparison. The prototype image, along with the time/size stamp, can help detect any tampering with original data.

Visual data archiving and indexing requires the implementation of efficient image retrieval algorithms. The number of shape-based image retrieval techniques has been rapidly increasing; however, currently there is no single technique that consistently maintains optimal performance in all image subsets of the database. Several successful techniques can combine to improve the retrieval process using fusion either on the classifier or feature level. Retrieval using fusion in the semantic system substantially improves the accuracy of querying.[12]

In visual data archiving and indexing, automatic object segmentation is necessary to handle the large number of images expected to populate the database. Using the system presented here, the analyst groups and indexes the segmented objects according to the semantically defined relational rules of the database. The rules enable the system to perform effective image registration and retrieval. The automation of segmenting objects from an image functions through a combination of adaptive thresholding and contour-based image matching. The relational object-oriented database uses a hierarchical data structure to complement the proposed system with needed speed and efficiency.

The semantic database includes many basic features about each particular object. The semantic features can form the basic structure that controls queries flowing into the database. The database is formed using a hierarchical tree structure. The database is capable of providing an xml link to each segmented object in each single image frame as well as the whole collections of frames that may form a video clip.

The classification of objects stored in the semantic database, as well as the retrieval of similar objects, works with one or more classifiers. Using more than one classifier may improve the retrieval process. The fusion process combines the classifiers based on assigning different weights to each classifier, giving greater emphasis to the more successful ones.

The number of shape-based image retrieval classifiers has been rapidly increasing; however, while each classifier has advantages, it also comes with a number of shortcomings. Some of these shortcomings can be overcome, but others should be completely abandoned. Methods that give a reasonable degree of robustness are often computationally complex. Akrem El-Ghazal *et al.*, proposed to fuse several of these techniques at the classification level to capitalize on their benefits and enhance the process of shape-based image retrieval.[13]

The main motivation behind this work is to select image retrieval techniques that capture the most relevant characteristics of an object in the most economical number of features to be included in the database. Unfortunately, no single method or technique could work for all kinds of objects or images. The optimal solution is to combine several techniques and make them collaborate to achieve the highest retrieval performance. In this essence, the best techniques compete to reach the final decision using statistical ranking or simply statistical fusion. This works by raising the rank of shapes that gets the highest votes among several classifiers. The analyst computes the shape ranks using the average or median ranks of a particular shape among all competing classifiers.

The evaluation of different shape-based image retrieval techniques is not an easy task due to the lack of a standard database. Researchers in this field tend to develop their own databases that are often limited in size and/or application scope. Many researches use the MPEG-7 as a substitute for standard image database.[14] A study, coauthored by Akrem El-Ghazal, Otman Basir, and Saeid Belkasim, implements fusion of classifiers including the Invariant Zernike Moments (ZMs).[15] ZMs, which are region-based and can provide global characteristics of a shape, outperform other global shape descriptors. Fusing several of the top shape retrieval techniques would improve the overall performance and outperform any individual technique. As evident from Table 8-1, fusion clearly improves the number of correctly matched shapes.

Method	Zernike Moments	Fourier Descriptors	Multi-Triangular Area	Classifier Fusion
Accuracy	59.16%	54.61%	60.01%	71.35%

Table 8-1. Effect of Classifier Fusion between Zernike Moments and Fourier Descriptors for Top 20 Matches.

The consensus-based fusion algorithm, sketched in Figure 8-5, aims to improve the retrieval performance of a group of shape-based image retrieval techniques by achieving consensus with respect to their rankings. Preliminary experimental results investigated the performance of the proposed algorithm using set B of the widely used MPEG-7 image database.

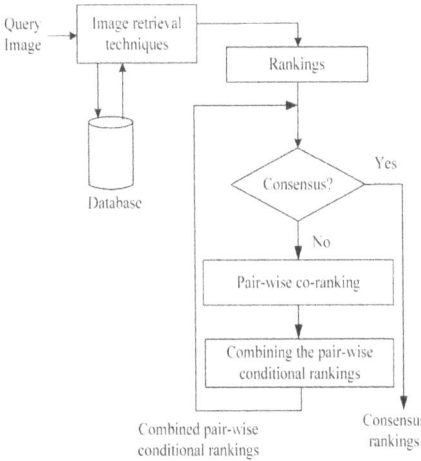

Figure 8-5. The Consensus-based Fusion Algorithm.

The experimental results shown in Figure 8-6 demonstrate that the proposed algorithm yields better results than does any of three other popular shape retrieval techniques. Furthermore, the performance of the proposed algorithm is superior to that produced by the three individual rankings. This improvement is the result of allowing the individual retrieval techniques to recursively exchange their ranking information until all the techniques reach a consensus about their rankings. The overall reported experimental results demonstrate the effectiveness of the proposed algorithm for image retrieval.

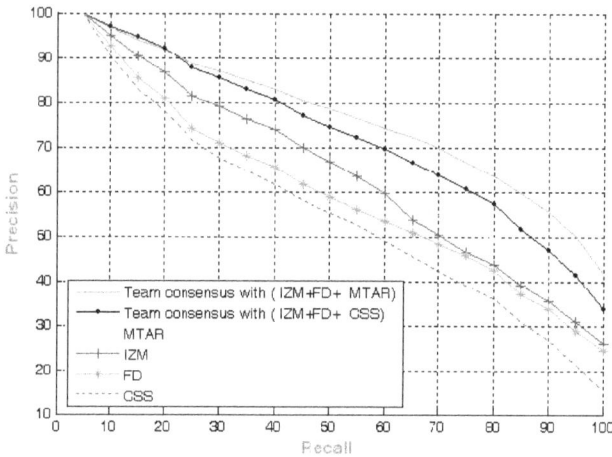

Figure 8-6. Comparison between Precision-Recall of the Fourier Descriptors, Zernike Moments, and Multi Triangular Area Techniques Using the Consensus-based Fusion Algorithm.

BENEFITS OF THE SEMANTIC DATABASE APPROACH

The Semantic Database Approach offers a preferred method of image retrieval for analysts of extremists' messages. Quantitative analysis and comparison of large collections of images under different conditions requires sophisticated statistical shape recognition and retrieval tools.[16] To begin with, implementing the system does not result in the loss of any of the benefits of the current syntactical approach. Instead, the semantic database builds on top of the syntactic approach to produce a complete semantic system. Analysts, if they prefer, can still retrieve images through sequential ordering by limiting the database's semantic rules for specific images. The complexity of the system depends on the size and the complexity of the semantic rules the analyst desires and programmers implement.[17]

The semantic approach also produces more efficient and more productive image retrieval. Particularly in cases where producers have modified the content of images, the semantic approach can increase their efficient retrieval. Relaxing the order requirements of the syntactic approach widens the matching process to include any image that has multiple symbols embedded within it. Reconsider the image described earlier that included three elements: a disc, a star, and a square. The semantic approach would tag any one of these constituent elements, expanding the retrieval mechanisms to more likely capture altered uses of the image. The relaxation of order restriction can also include relations between successive items, making image frames manipulated within videos easier to detect. Empirical testing reveals that the semantic database is useful for extracting hidden patterns or discovering new trends.[18]

The semantic relations in the database are completely independent and detachable from their associated images; therefore they can be partially retrieved from their image. This property enables retrieval based on certain requirements that may not be satisfied in the whole image but can be partially satisfied in one or few objects in the same image or multiple images. A video may contain several key objects distributed over more than one image; the programmer would then use the semantic relation to link these objects.

The semantic database also provides effective retrieval support for multiple formats of data. The semantic relational database can incorporate input data from many other sources such as audio input, test and other meta-data. The system's semantic rules can be flexible enough to adapt to visual and/or nonvisual relations between its constitutive elements. The fact that the image object can be semantically related to other variable format objects enriches the depth of analysis possible from the retrieval system. A unified database that ties all items in a more comprehensive way will permit analysts to reach more informed conclusions about the vast propaganda efforts in the online environment.

A final notable benefit of the semantic database approach is the ease and productivity of its ongoing refinements. The unified semantic database approach offers a user-friendly platform that accommodates all inputs from experts across different disciplines by enriching the system and enabling it to serve as an expert system that improves the overall performance. The system can evolve by incorporating semantic rules based on the interpretations of others who traditionally are noncomputer scientists. With the semantic database approach, the computer scientist provides the initial tools for retrieving, archiving, and analyzing data, while content experts analyze the data and modify or suggest new models for categorizing or extracting certain trends or patterns.

Such collaboration has the potential to bring new visions and offer solutions to problems that may not be solvable otherwise. The idea here is to translate the rules put by the users to the algorithms, not the algorithms to the users. Using such an approach, a content expert could greatly benefit from the system and modify it at any time, which allows the system to evolve and become smarter as more user feedback is incorporated into it. A set of visual communication rules based on experimental results developed by content experts could further refine the automated system and improve the computer analysis stage.

Analysts can further refine the semantic rules of images by conducting experiments on recording interactions of a group of users with the layout of different components of a single image or multiple image frames within one or several videos. The obvious benefit of video semantics is the transformation of a rigid system into a dynamically evolving one. The system becomes robust as the time progresses, while analysts tailor the semantic rules to agree with results of field studies.

In sum, the collaborative nature of the semantic rule approach improves the effectiveness of tracking extremist postings and increases the accuracy of the standard image retrieval algorithms. The inclusion of pattern analysis with the semantic database enables the detection of any hidden messages that are implicitly embedded within many popular images or videos. The incorporation of text, image, and audio characteristics into one standardized multimedia retrieval system is naturally adaptable to, and maximizes the benefits of, the semantic database.

ENDNOTES - CHAPTER 8

1. "Dark Web Terrorism Research," Tempe, AZ: University of Research," available from *www.ai.arizona.edu/research/terror/*, accessed on November 29, 2012.

2. "Internet 2011 in Numbers," *Pingdom*, January 12, 2012, available from *www.royal.pingdom.com /2012/01/17/internet-2011-in-numbers/*, accessed on November 29, 2012.

3. Marshall Soules, "Images and Propaganda: From the Sacred to the Profane," *Media Studies*, July 1, 2012, available from *www.media-studies.ca/articles.htm*; Claire Stokoe, "100 Years Of Propaganda: The Good, The Bad and The Ugly," *Smashing Magazine*, June 13, 2010, available from *www.smashingmagazine. com/2010/06/13/100-years-of-propaganda-the-good-the-bad-and-the-ugly/*.

4. Ashwini V. Malviya and S. A. Ladhake, "A Review on Passive Approach for Image Manipulation Detection Techniques for Copy Move Forgery," *Journal of Computing Technologies*, Vol. 2, Issue 1, June 2012.

5. James O'Brien and Hany Farid, "Exposing Photo Manipulation with Inconsistent Reflections," *ACM Transactions on Graphics*, Vol. 31, No. 1, 2012, pp. 4:1-11.

6. Mikihiro Ioka, "A Method of Defining the Similarity of Images on the Basis of Color Information," *Technical Report RT-0030*, Tokyo, Japan: IBM Research Laboratory, 1989; Jie Huang, "Image Indexing Using Color Correlogram," *IEEE Int. Conference on Computer Vision and Pattern Recognition*, Puerto Rico, 1997, pp. 762-768.

7. Jiang Yang, Chong Wah Ngo, and Yang Jae, "Towards Optimal Bag-of-Features for Object Categorization and Semantic Video Retrieval," *Proceedings of ACM International Conference on Image and Video Retrieval*, 2007, pp. 494-501.

8. *Ibid*; Jun Yang, Chong-Wah Ngo, and Alexander G. Hauptmann, "Representations of Keypoint-Based Semantic Concept Detection: A Comprehensive Study," *IEEE Transactions on Multimedia*, Vol. 12, Issue 1, January 2010, pp. 42–53.

9. W. Frei and C. C. Chen, "Fast Boundary Detection: A Generalization and a New Algorithm," *IEEE Transaction Computer*, Vol. C-26, No. 10, 1977, pp. 988-998; John Canny, "A Computational Approach to Edge Detection," *IEEE Transactions on Pattern Analysis and Machine Intelligence*, Vol. 8, Issue 6, 1986, pp. 679-698.

10. Saeid O. Belkasim, Xiangu Hong, and Otman Badir, "Content Based Image Retrieval Using Discrete Wavelet Transform,"

International Journal of Pattern Recognition and Artificial Intelligence, Vol. 18, No. 1, 2004, pp. 19-32; Saeid O. Belkasim, Yong Li, Erdogan Dogdu, Xiangu Hong, and Z. Li, "Contented-Based Image Retrieval in Biological Databases," presented at the *International Conference on Computational Intelligence,* Istanbul, Turkey, 2004, pp. 512-515.

11. Ioka, 1989; Huang, 1997.

12. Akrem El-Ghazal, Otman Basir, and Saeid Belkasim, "A Consensus-based Fusion Algorithm in Shape-based Image Retrieval," presented at the *10th International Conference on Information Fusion,* April 2007; Akrem El-Ghazal, Otman Basir, and Saeid Belkasim, "A New Shape Signature for Fourier Descriptors," Proceedings of the *IEEE International Conference on Image Processing,* 2007; Akrem El-Ghazal, Otman Basir, and Saeid Belkasim, "Shape-Based Image Retrieval Using Pair-wise Candidate Co-ranking," presented at the *International Conference on Image Analysis and Recognition,* April 2007.

13. El-Ghazal, Basir, and Belkasim, "A Consensus-based Fusion Algorithm in Shape-based Image Retrieval"; El-Ghazal, Basir, and Belkasim, "A New Shape Signature for Fourier Descriptors"; El-Ghazal, Basir, and Belkasim, "Shape-Based Image Retrieval Using Pair-wise Candidate Co-ranking."

14. Farzin Mokhtarian and Miroslaw Bober, *Curvature Scale Space Representation: Theory Application and MPEG-7 Standardization,* New York: Springer, 2003.

15. Alireza Khotanzad and Yaw Hua Hong, "Invariant Image Recognition by Zernike Moments," *IEEE Transactions on Pattern Analysis and Machine Intelligence,* Vol. 12, No. 1, 1990, pp. 489-497; Ye Bin and Peng Jia-xiong, "Improvement and invariance analysis of Zernike Moments Using as a Region-based Shape Descriptor," *XV Brazilian Symposium on Computer Graphics and Image Processing,* 2002, pp. 120-127; Akrem El-Ghazal, Otman Basir, and Saeid Belkasim, ""Multi-Descriptor Fusion for Shape-based Image Retrieval," *Journal of Advances in Information Fusion,* 2012.

16. Saeid O. Belkasim, Malayappan Shridhar, and Majid Ahmadi, "New Methods for Contour Detection and Automatic

Thresholding," *Canadian Journal of Electronic & Computing*, Vol. 20, No. 4, 1995, pp. 57-81; Akrem El-Ghazal, Otman Basir, and Saeid Belkasim, "Invariant Curvature-Based Shape Descriptors," *Journal of Visual Communication and Image Representation*, 2012; Akrem El-Ghazal, Otman Basir, and Saeid Belkasim, "Farthest Point Distance: A New Shape Signature for Fourier Descriptors," *Signal Processing: Image Communication*, Vol. 24, Issue 7, August 2009, pp. 572-586.

17. Fausto Giunchiglia, Uladzimir Kharkevich, and Ilya Zaihrayeu, "Concept Search," York Sure and John Domingue, eds., *The Semantic Web: Research and Applications: 3rd European Semantic Web Conference, June 11-14, 2006, Proceedings*, New York: Springer, 2006, pp. 429-444.

18. Saeid O. Belkasim, Malayappan Shridhar, and Majid Ahmadi, "Pattern Recognition with Moment Invariants: A Comparative Study and New Results," *Pattern Recognition*, Vol. 24, 1991, pp. 1117-1138; Saeid O. Belkasim, E. Hassan, and T. Obeidi, "Radial Zernike Moment Invariants," *4th International Conference on Computer and Information Technology*, Wuhan, China, 2004, pp. 14-16; Saeid O. Belkasim, Ahmed Ghazal, and Otman Basir, "Edge Enhanced Optimum Automatic Thresholding," *Proceedings of the 2000 International Computer Symposium*, Taiwan, December 6-8, 2000, pp. 78-86.

CHAPTER 9

BIG PICTURES AND VISUAL PROPAGANDA: THE LESSONS OF RESEARCH ON THE "EFFECTS" OF PHOTOJOURNALISTIC ICONS

Natalia Mielczarek
David D. Perlmutter

Representational pictures were the first true "medium" our ancestors created, some 30,000-40,000 years ago. Some of the early pictures were accurate depictions of the natural world. Others likely had a persuasive, even political, intent as they employed deliberate factual distortions.[1] Understanding this human factor is crucial in understanding pictures. Any estimation of the meaning or effects of a picture must take into account the receptivity, attitudes, and beliefs of audiences, as well as those of producers or disseminators. For example, analysts cannot treat, interpret, or dismiss pro-terrorism pictures — however one defines terrorism — simply as "propaganda." For some, such images are indeed politically charged misinformation; for others, they are self-evidently news with high degrees of veridicality and verisimilitude.

In this chapter, we present a review of the scholarly literature on the impact that famous news photographs exert on individuals, public opinion, and policy decisions.[2] Research on this topic spans various academic fields — from psychology to mass communication — and straddles both qualitative and quantitative methods of inquiry. We address the ascribed powers of news pictures by singling out the so-called "big pictures," or super icons, as metonyms of broader events and emotions. Not accidentally, these images are also the kinds of pictures political entities from governments to terrorist organizations are most likely to use to achieve their persuasive purposes.

Specifically, here we systematically address popular conceptions about ascribed powers of news pictures and provide a broader context for their interpretation. We critique the popular view, because often the cumulative research evidence paints a very different picture of the "power" of pictures. We then make suggestions for the application of our conclusions toward the study of extremist visual propaganda.

NOT ALL PICTURES ARE EQUAL

Innumerable stimuli inundate the sensory cortices of modern humans each day, including thousands of artificially produced or mediated pictures, from cat videos on YouTube, to billboard ads along the road, to sitcoms on television, to news photos in magazines. Our minds, however, do not treat each visual image equally. Some pictures, emergent as photo or photojournalistic "icons," seem to stand out, become famous and popular, and remain in a common wellspring of reference. Such famous pictures tend to encapsulate the phenomena and emotions they depict.[3] Merely state the words "Iwo Jima" or "Tiananmen," for example, and certain individual frames or short film/video clips spring *from* our mind: They do so because they have been planted there via many viewings. Whatever other powers photo icons have—and we will argue that pictures have potential powers, not one uniform superpower—their ability to "stand for" large, complicated events is a commonplace.

Photo and news editors function as visual news gatekeepers in the process of icon determination.[4]

They, together with photographers, choose only a handful of pictures that end up published or aired. Their selection decisions are not objective. The gatekeepers single out pictures according to preconceived ideas of beauty, composition strength, conceptions of reality, and assumptions of what pictures would appeal to audience members, their employers, and peers. The "wow factor" is among the central criteria for selection because it presumably captures the attention of the viewer. More specifically, emotions, celebrities in the picture, technique, and unexpectedness are among the key factors that photo editors evaluate when they make decisions about which pictures from a lineup will end up in print, on television, or now online.[5] Ideology is also a driving force in the process of selection for pictures for public consumption, as pictures appear often because somebody finds them useful.[6]

THE MYTH (AND REALITY) OF THE BIG PICTURE

We often hear about "pictures that changed the world." The central claim of this lay theory of visual determinism is that pictures can magically "stop a war" or "drive public opinion." Visual determinism grants news pictures the mighty power to influence public opinion and prompt policy changes. Presidents, foreign policy experts, pundits, and journalists generously have dispensed such sweeping pronouncements but have rarely backed up those claims with anything more than anecdotal evidence. Today, a large gap exists in social scientific research examining the direct impact of pictures on policy.

In offering this critique of visual determinism, we do not claim that pictures produce zero effect.[7] In fact, the power of pictures works in various ways. Certainly, specific news photographs have moved people. Pictures of the Civil Rights movement and of deep poverty in Sao Paulo, Brazil, triggered an outpouring of donations to both causes,[8] demonstrating that people can and do respond to photographs, but on a smaller scale than what enthusiasts of visual determinism would have us believe. Evidence also suggests that war pictures may impact people's attitudes. News photographs from the 2003 Iraq war that depicted casualties and were accompanied by captions elicited more negative emotions than written accounts of the same content alone.[9] What is more, after looking at the same news photographs with captions, readers said their support for America's prolonged involvement in the conflict had diminished.

Further conclusions about the lasting effects of such opinion shifts, however, need more research before their findings extrapolate to other contexts. Here, we simply caution about making broad generalizations that imply a causal directionality of effect without rigorous investigation to determine the strength of support for such assertions. Extraordinary claims must have as their foundation extraordinary evidence; photo icons are not exempt from this scientific dictum. In sum, the weight of evidence suggests that (a) picture effects depend on multiple factors besides the persuasive content embedded in the picture itself, (b) many assumptions about the impact of pictures have their origins in popular legends rather than scientifically investigated cases, and (c) when scholars do examine real-world picture effects, the impacts prove much more nuanced than the ascribed picture-as-hypodermic-needle scenario.

BELIEVING IS SEEING . . .
AND THE BELIEVER'S POWER COUNTS

One popular myth is that pictures do not lie, and further that they have a fixed meaning. Here again, the audience context confounds such a simplistic cause-and-effect scenario. First, pictures depend highly on captions and contextual information for their meaning. Whether a photo has the caption "Serbian civilians killed by Bosnian Muslims" or "Bosnian Muslim civilians killed by Serbians" radically changes the way viewers may perceive the image, although the photo remains the same. The captioning of a picture, either physically in the news stream or mentally by our pre-conceptions of it, can radically change the image's meaning for us. To take the most bipolar dichotomy: One man's atrocity photo may be another man's trophy snapshot. Perpetrators produced most of the visual depictions of the World War II Holocaust of European Jews, for example, for reasons ranging from record keeping to touristic curiosity.

Thus, the processes of reading and interpreting news photographs do not occur in a cognitive or emotional vacuum. People interpret what they see through the prism of a media climate that discourse elites, such as journalists and political leaders, shape to serve their own interests. Humans, conditioned from infancy to favor seeing over our other senses, ascribe generally to the notion that "what we see is what we get."[10] Consequently, people tend to take photographs at face value and believe that what they see is the truth.[11] That said, the human mind has almost infinite capacities to ignore the truth when it wants to do so.

The idea of "seeing is believing" becomes even more problematic in the digital age.[12] Historically, photographs and film functioned as the closest possible representation of reality, but digital manipulation has left photography as open to question as any other medium. In his survey of digital alteration of images in the service of propaganda, Scot Macdonald notes:

> Today, those who produce propaganda and practice deception based on pictures no longer even have to start with reality. Computers allow the creation of any imaginable picture, still or moving.[13]

Manipulated pictures online "create an altered reality for the viewer and provide a powerful weapon to those who will practice propaganda and deception."[14] Governments have used such manipulated pictures to prop up deception operations in politics, diplomacy, and war.

When we look at news photographs, we do not analyze them in a contextual vacuum without the weight of our prior experience.[15] Perlmutter and Wagner, in their study of the making of a photojournalistic icon, assert that:

> What we are allowed to see has socio-political importance because mental schemas can be established and activated by the frames through which media represent issues, events and persons in the news and even by the mere choice of determining a topic newsworthy.[16]

Information processing models within cognitive theory of mind in psychology suggest that what we see develops meaning in the context of what we have seen before and what we have stored in our long-term memory.[17] Much of what we think about when we see a picture stems from our subjectivity and guides our interpretation.[18] Each news picture we see works on several levels, from literal and symbolic to personal, cultural, and timeless.[19]

The key point for both researchers and the public is that the interpretation of a photograph involves more than just the picture itself. Consider the "first person effect" where a powerful military or political leader shapes policy because he or she assumes a picture affects other people (often as in "the people" or "the press"). The picture, as a result, indirectly acquires a truly powerful effect, not because the image actually changed any minds, but because a key decisionmaker assumed that it would impact public opinion and acted in anticipation of that effect. The picture thus creates a self-fulfilling prophecy.

The most famous example of first-person dynamics in wartime came at the end – indeed may have caused the end – of the first Gulf War in 1991.[20] The fear that "bad" pictures might overturn the supportive public mood for the war effort resulted in the conflict's termination; in retrospect, considering Saddam Hussein's survival, this was premature at least in terms of American policy objectives. In his autobiography, Colin Powell explicitly states that he made policy based on assumptions that "other" people – the press, the American public, Arab allies – would be affected by pictures:

> Saddam had ordered his forces to withdraw from Kuwait. The last major escape route, a four-lane highway leading out of Kuwait City toward the Iraqi city of Basrah, had turned into a shooting gallery for our fliers. The road was choked with fleeing soldiers and littered with the charred hulks of nearly 1,500 military

and civilian vehicles. Reporters began referring to this road as the 'Highway of Death'. I would have to give the President and the Secretary [of Defense Dick Cheney] a recommendation soon as to when to stop, I told Norm [Schwarzkopf]. The television coverage, I added, was starting to make it look as if we were engaged in slaughter for slaughter's sake.[21]

"Look" is the key verb; the "Basra road of death" was, in retrospect, a misnomer. Two giant Iraqi convoys streamed north from Kuwait on February 25. Land- and sea-based coalition planes encountered no resistance as they raided the long lines of vehicles day and night; pilots likened it to strafing "Daytona Beach on spring break."[22] Yet, subsequent estimates put the Iraqi casualty figures as very low in proportion to the amount of visible material destruction: a few hundred to 1,000 soldiers killed, much fewer than in previous operations of the air war, or indeed of most air wars.[23] As journalist Michael Kelly pointed out, the awesome American firepower scared off the drivers and riders; most of the vehicles bombed were probably abandoned.[24] But from the air, even from a close distance, a several-mile-long column of burned-out trucks and cars obscured any body count. From the point of view of public relations, the image looking like a slaughter was more important than whether it really was. The gutted machinery became a metonym of human carnage.

Some pictures of charred bodies and vehicles on the Basra road did make it into the media. However, whether such a visualized slaughter would really have upset a U.S. public primed and inclined to hate Saddam Hussein, disdain Arabs, support U.S. troops, and appreciate a relatively quick and bloodless (for the United States) victory remains unclear. In short, hindsight suggests that Colin Powell was worrying unnecessarily about the power of pictures, but that conclusion is the point. *Pictures unquestionably have power over leaders when they assume the same pictures will have power over others, including voters and the press.* The perception of the threat of "bad" pictures can be a check on modern political and military thought and behavior, especially in an age when governments have less than absolute control over the pictures that appear in the international news stream.

Finally, not all audiences are equally important or influential in assessing the power of pictures. A picture that weakens the will (which may have been weakening already) of a war leader to the point of giving him reason to change a policy may, in fact, have minor effects on many other audiences. Such was the case with the 1968 news photograph of the so-called "Saigon execution" that Associated Press photographer Eddie Adams shot during the Tet Offensive. The picture captures the moment just as Nguyen Ngoc Loan, chief of the South Vietnamese National Police, shoots a "Viet Cong suspect" in the head. A 1976 study by scholars George Bailey and Lawrence Lichty measured, in part, NBC viewers' reaction to the news film of the same event that the Huntley-Brinkley Report broadcast.[25] The iconic picture that supposedly shocked and outraged audiences to where the U.S. Government changed its policy in Vietnam elicited merely 90 letters to NBC. Most of them (62 percent) were complaints about the network's poor taste in airing such footage. More than 30 came from parents of young children, protesting that the broadcast might have exposed their kids to the gruesome pictures. If these pictures really had such a strong impact, we think there would have been greater evidence for it.

Another study of the Saigon execution photo-graph, conducted as part of the famous "Middletown" Indiana opinion research project, further reveals that claims about the impact of Adams' photo on audiences have been exaggerated.[26] An examination of three local newspapers' coverage of the Vietnam War, coupled with interviews of local citizens, found diverse responses to the conflict. Within weeks of the Tet Offensive, the study concluded, other issues drew the attention of the subjects.

As one of the authors of this chapter determined in his study of the Saigon execution, while the picture may indeed have had an effect on a demoralized *president*, a large majority of the American public, whose main wartime concerns were the mortality and casualty rate of U.S. servicemen, the costs and length of the war, and the unlikelihood of outright victory, did not have a strong reaction to the fate of a single communist enemy.[27]

POWERS, NOT POWER, OF PICTURES

Asserting that a picture or group of pictures is powerful may be popular but remains scientifically imprecise. We read in newspapers, magazines, and books that certain pictures are powerful in that they possess the power to move us and to change our minds. Such claims often come close to making it sound like pictures have a single superpower, which seems to operate in one specific way. But we suggest that pictures can have several powers at the same time, or some but not others. They may, for example, move us aesthetically — like the Saigon execution — but have no or little lasting political power. They may work as metonyms for an event to telescope or sum up a cause, era, or happening, but have no (long-term) effect on governmental policy.

TOWARD COUNTERMEASURES

Like researchers in general, we believe our topic needs more research from many disciplinary approaches and with varying methods. Experimental, observation, survey, and field studies could examine productively (a) how certain kinds of audiences, from policymakers to targeted recruiting populations, react to visual stimuli of various kinds, and (b) the conditions for how they then act (or do not act) upon such stimuli. That said, we think the multidisciplinary research evidence has strong, if preliminary, implications for anyone trying to understand the power(s) of images, especially those we label "extremist." Specifically, those concerned with creating counter-messaging approaches should follow a social-cognitive strategy. By this, we mean that such analysts should not isolate pictures from the society and beliefs of the population under study.

First and foremost, we should ask what social-cognitive system functions in the minds of the beholders of such images. Pictures do not affect anyone in a vacuum or onto a blank slate. If, as we argue, available evidence supports "believing is seeing," then researchers asking what effects a particular visual stimulus (like an iconic photo) or stimuli (like a genre of such photos) have on a person or a group should consider the subjects' beliefs about the relevant topic.

Second, we should appreciate that people have tremendous capacity to edit images and alter their meanings. More than a century of social cognition research shows that we tend to seek out data that supports

our pre-existing beliefs, suppress data that may contradict them, and even recast data from one category
to another. The more ingrained the belief, the more it
touches our self-esteem, the more likely it will be hard
to budge, no matter what new evidence comes along.

General belief systems, however, do change on the
societal and individual level. Conflicts do not *naturally*
exist across time. A thousand years ago, most Euro-
peans, and indeed many Arabs, would have concluded that those originating in Norway, Denmark, and
Sweden were inherently violent and predatory to a
psychotic degree. Today, few, if any, people associate
Scandinavians with such traits. Likewise, the general
Japanese or German attitude toward war and conquest noticeably changed between 1938 and 1946. The
thinking of people is not static, and so any research
on, for example, "what Muslim teens believe" has to
be reexamined periodically to keep current with new
developments.

Although people can be quite tenacious in holding
onto beliefs, even those that seem to others fantastic or
unsupported by actual evidence, an array of scientifically supported techniques to "debunk" false beliefs
exists.[28] Many of these techniques remain little known
and are often counterintuitive. For example, when
people face a long, exhaustive list of arguments and
evidence why their belief on a topic is wrong, they
mentally "dig in," rejecting the new stimuli, and even
reinterpreting the points as reinforcing their original
beliefs. On the other hand, a few short examples may
have power to change a mind. More research is needed on the role visuals may have on such purposive
persuasion.

The most pointed targets of radical propaganda
of all kinds are young, based on the assumption that

young people are the most malleable in their beliefs and preferences. To be sure, youth—predominantly male youth—have the potential for exponential violence. Indeed, the executioners in every genocidal act, and most acts of mass terror in history, have been young males, often recruited by propaganda, visual or otherwise. But young people can also mobilize to save whales, research cures for disease, and die nobly for their homeland. They steer toward darkness or light depending on who and what is able to influence them.

In any complex system, competing ideas and beliefs exist alongside movements urging the translation of those concepts into action. Attempts to counter radicalizing propaganda, visual or otherwise, should not appear via external Western imposition. Rather, more productive avenues include alliances and encouragement with indigenous movements that try to create underlying belief systems that are beneficial to all countries, cultures, and civilizations. Western governments and institutions seeking to create countermeasures against radical anti-Western propaganda, visual and otherwise, will likely fail if enacted without local input and cooperation.

We think opportunities are available for forming alliances in combating terrorism. First, we should note that such unions do not need to focus exclusively on partners who agree on every point of policy and ideology. For example, in the wide and very diverse Muslim world—which, of course, includes many Muslim adherents of a variety of sects living in countries not predominately Muslim—innumerable individuals, governments, and groups oppose violent terrorism. During the *Visual Propaganda and Online Radicalization Conference*,[29] scholars repeatedly noted that, in the case of "lone wolf" terrorists in the West, their radicalization seemed to have as a proximate cause web-based (often visual) al-Qaeda created or sympathetic propaganda. At the same time, many of the lone wolves failed in their intentions and found themselves subject to arrest because family members, most often their parents, turned them in to authorities. We suggest that, especially in Western countries, an obvious general area of partnership would be with parents expressing concern about their children taking destructive and self-destructive paths.

Second, to go to the other end of the spectrum, very large Muslim movements also are definitively opposed to terroristic violence; are pro-dialogue and discussion; and already have their own educational mechanisms, networks, and institutions. The most prominent of these, with which David Perlmutter, one of the authors of this chapter, has worked for almost a decade, is the Hizmet movement, inspired by Turkish philosopher and cleric Fethullah Gülen. Gülen's followers number possibly in the tens of millions. Their associated foundations, charities, and societies have set up schools, think tanks, cultural exchanges, discussion groups, and conferences across the globe. Although Gülen is controversial in his native Turkey, where the secular/religious divide is an extremely politically sensitive one, in the opinion of many others, he functions as a tremendously positive force for establishing a nonviolent doctrine of Islamic thought and practice. Similar movements would be key players in any large-scale attempt to counter destructive propaganda of any type, but particularly that purportedly inspired by Islam.

As we have argued, humanization may not be as powerful as some think when it resides in the photo icon. Human beings have remarkable abilities to ignore the suffering of those whom they do not like. Sustained programs of one-on-one contact, or lengthy personal engagement, or even hearing directly from others we see as enemies about the origins of their attitudes can be extremely helpful. During the visual propaganda conference, participants discussed many times how participants from the Middle East, Europe, and the United States were often not familiar with images used in others' data sets. Is it quite possible to grow up and hear only about the suffering of one's own group? Simply hearing about the suffering of others, especially as part of a sustained educational program, may help provide greater understanding and context.

To conclude, the study of photo icons reveals that the powers of pictures on audiences are complex and under-researched. To move forward, any study of visual propaganda and radicalization should take into account the cognition, culture, society, and context around a picture. To study the image, we must study the world from which the image originates and the world that the viewer encounters.

ENDNOTES - CHAPTER 9

1. David D. Perlmutter, *Visions of War: Picturing Warfare from the Stone Age to the Cyberage*, New York: St. Martin's Griffin, 1999.

2. David D. Perlmutter, *Photojournalism and Foreign Policy: Icons of Outrage in International Crises*, Westport, CT: Praeger, 1998; David D. Perlmutter and Nicole Smith Dahmen, "(In)visible Evidence: Pictorially Enhanced Disbelief in the Apollo Moon Landings," *Visual Communication*, Vol. 7, No. 2, May 2008, pp. 229-251; Lesa Hatley Major and David D. Perlmutter, "The Fall of a Pseudo-icon: The Toppling of Saddam Hussein's Statue as Picture Management," *Visual Communication Quarterly*, Vol. 12, No. 1-2, 2005, pp. 38-45; David D. Perlmutter, "The Internet: Big Pictures and Interactors"; Larry Gross, John Stuart Katz, and Jay

Ruby, eds., *Picture Ethics in the Digital Age*, Minneapolis, MN: University of Minnesota Press, 2004, pp. 1-26; David D. Perlmutter and Gretchen Wagner, "The Anatomy of a Photojournalistic Icon: Marginalization of Dissent in the Selection and Framing of 'A Death in Genoa'," *Visual Communication*, Vol. 3, No. 1, February 2004, pp. 91-107; David Domke, David D. Perlmutter, and Meg Spratt, "The Primes of Our Times? An Examination of the 'Power' of Visual Pictures," *Journalism*, Vol. 3, No. 2, August 2002, pp. 131-159; David D. Perlmutter, "Manufacturing Visions of Society and History in Textbooks," *Journal of Communication*, Vol. 47, No. 3, Summer 1997, pp. 68-81; David D. Perlmutter, "Remembering the 'Big Picture': A Photojournalistic Icon of the Iraq War in the 'IDS' Age," Ralph D. Berenger, ed., *Cybermedia Go to War: Role of Converging Media During and After the 2003 Iraq War*, Spokane, WA: Marquette Books, 2006, pp. 340-360; David D. Perlmutter, "Hypericons: Famous News Pictures in the Internet-Digital-Satellite Age," Paul Messaris, ed., *Digital Media: Transformations in Human Communication*, New York: Peter Lang, 2006, pp. 51-64.

3. Perlmutter and Wagner, p. 100.

4. Kimberly Bissell, "Culture and Gender as Factors in Photojournalism Gatekeeping," *Visual Communication Quarterly*, Vol. 7, No. 2, 2000, pp. 9-12; Kimberly Bissell, "A Return to Mr. Gates: Photography and Objectivity," *Newspaper Research Journal*, Vol. 2, 2000b, pp. 81-93; Michelle Seelig: "A Case for the Visual Elite," *Visual Communication Quarterly*, Vol. 12, No. 3-4, 2000, pp. 164-181.

5. Patrick Rossler, Jana Bomhoff, Josef Ferdinand Haschke, Jan Kersten, and Rudiger Muller, "Selection and Impact of Press Photography: An Empirical Study on the Basis of Photo News Factor," *Communications*, Vol. 36, No. 4, 2011, pp. 415-439.

6. Perlmutter and Wagner, pp. 100-101.

7. Donald D. Hoffman, *Visual Intelligence: How We Create What We See*, New York: W. W. Norton, 1998.

8. Vicki Goldberg, *The Power of Photography*, New York: Abbeville Press, 1991; Tom Koch, *The News as Myth: Fact and Context in Journalism*, New York: Greenwood Press, 1990.

9. Michael Pfau, Michael Haigh, Andeelynn Fifrick, Douglas Holl, Allison Tedesco, Jay Cope, David Nunnally, Amy Schiess, Donald Preston, Paul Roszkowski, and Marlon Martin, "The Effects of Print News Photographs of the Casualties of War," *Journalism & Mass Communication Quarterly*, Vol. 83, No. 1, March 2006, pp. 150-168.

10. Alan Dundes, "Seeing is Believing," Carol Lowery Delaney, ed., *Investigating Culture: An Experimental Introduction to Anthropology*, Malden, MA: Blackwell Publishing, 2004, pp. 170-174.

11. Doris Graber: "Television News Without Pictures?" *Critical Studies in Mass Communication*, Vol. 4, No. 1, 1987, pp. 85-96.

12. Scot Macdonald, *Propaganda and Information Warfare in the Twenty-first Century: Altered Pictures and Deception Operations*, New York: Routledge, 2007.

13. *Ibid.*, p. 1.

14. *Ibid.*, p. 3.

15. Perlmutter and Wagner, p. 104.

16. *Ibid.*, p. 102.

17. Alan Baddeley: "Working Memory," *Science*, Vol. 255, 1992, pp. 556-559; "Exploring the Central Executive," *The Quarterly Journal of Experimental Psychology: A Human Experimental Psychology*, Vol. 49A, 1996, pp. 5-28; "The Central Executive: A Concept and Some Misconceptions," *Journal of the International Neuropsychological Society*, Vol. 4, 1998, pp. 523-526; "The Episodic Buffer: A New Component of Working Memory?" *Trends in Cognitive Sciences*, Vol. 4, 2000, pp. 417-423; "Working Memory: Looking Back and Looking Forward," *Nature Reviews Neuroscience*, Vol. 4, 2003, pp. 829-839.

18. Robert Craig, "Fact, Public Opinion, and Persuasion: The Rise of the Visual in Journalism and Advertising," Bonnie Brennen and Hanno Hardt, eds., *Picturing the Past: Media, History & Photography*, Urbana and Chicago, IL: University of Illinois Press, 1999, pp. 36-59; Leonard Berkowitz and Karen Rogers, "A Prim-

ing Effect Analysis of Media Influences," Jennings Bryant and Dolf Zillman, eds., *Perspectives on Media Effects*, Hillsdale, NJ: Lawrence Erlbaum Associates, 1986, pp. 57-82; Susan Fiske and Patricia Linville: "What Does the Concept Schema Buy Us?" *Personality and Social Psychology Bulletin*, Vol. 6, No. 4, December 1980, pp. 543-547.

19. Ann Marie Barry, *Visual Intelligence: Perception, Picture, and Manipulation in Visual Communication*, Albany, NY: State University of New York Press, 1997.

20. Recounted from (and original citations found in) Perlmutter, *Photojournalism and Foreign Policy: Icons of Outrage in International Crises*.

21. Colin Powell and Joseph E. Persico, *My American Journey*, New York: Ballantine Books, 1995, p. 505.

22. Perlmutter, *Photojournalism and Foreign Policy: Icons of Outrage in International Crises*.

23. *Ibid*.

24. Quoted in *Ibid*.

25. George Bailey and Lawrence Lichty: "Rough Justice on a Saigon Street: A Gatekeeping Study of NBC's Tet Execution Film," *Journalism Quarterly*, Vol. 49, No. 2, June 1972, pp. 221-229.

26. Anthony Edmonds, "The Tet Offensive and Middletown: A Study in Contradiction," Marc J. Gilbert and William Head, eds., *The Tet Offensive*, Westport, CT: Praeger Publishers, 1996, pp. 135-142.

27. John E. Mueller, *War, Presidents and Public Opinion*, New York: John Wiley and Sons, 1973.

28. John Cook and Stephen Lewandowsky, *The Debunking Handbook*, St. Lucia, Australia: University of Queensland, 2011.

29. *Visual Propaganda and Online Radicalization Conference*, hosted by Georgia State University in conjunction with the U.S. Army War College, on March 14-16, 2012, in Atlanta, GA.

CHAPTER 10

RESPONSES AND RECOMMENDATIONS

Cori E. Dauber
Louis H. Jordan, Jr.

Visual images need to be accounted for strategically, both through the monitoring of enemy visuals and through an awareness of how enemy propaganda can make visual use of the actions of U.S. and allied forces. Secretary of Defense Leon Panetta did not go far enough in May 2012, when, after a series of embarrassing images associated with forces in Afghanistan became international headlines, he chastised "the few who will do stupid things, who make misjudgments and [show] bad judgment." The enemy, who is increasingly technologically savvy, will manipulate images of U.S. forces and their original context. For example, the Taliban and the Islamic Group of Uzbekistan (IMU) recast news footage of Barack Obama's visit to the Wailing Wall in 2008. The candidate's message of respect and humility was recast into one of subservience. In short, the intended message is not always the reported message.

But even when something "stupid" occurs, an overarching visual response strategy must generate options that will counter effectively the visual narrative that our adversaries will inevitably spin. Take the examples of the picture of Marine personnel urinating on dead insurgents or those showing U.S. personnel in "Trophy Shot" positions. In all of these cases, three separate "stupid" things occurred: the act itself, the taking of a photographic image memorializing the act, and the distribution of the image to the media, making it ready source material for the enemy.

Leadership and planners must be prepared to re-spond to a "stupid" event that produces offending images — or even to a run of the mill or an intelligent event which adversaries can recast into images that work to the detriment of the United States and her allies. This volume provides many important insights that should inform the development of the military's visual response strategies. The authors rely on current research from communication studies, marketing, psychology, journalism, mass media, history, computer science, and other fields, as well as data-driven assessments of extremists' online practices, in order to offer guidance to the military community. Their insights challenge existing notions of how leaders should apologize for offending images, rethink counter-narratives and branding strategies, provide important understandings of the visual strategies of extremist groups at home and abroad, re-envision audiences in the online environment, and develop retrieval methods for online images that will permit the creation of better techniques for those charged with countering enemy propaganda going forward, especially in the information operations (IO) and military information support operations (MISO) communities. As this volume makes clear, a substantial and growing body of research has explored the impact of visual images, and increasingly, the way they function in the online environment.

The core and consensus assumptions of that work, where applicable to force readiness, needs to be integrated at all levels of training. Such training should expand beyond those in the public affairs (PA), MISO, and IO communities; it should also reach those in command positions to support thinking about visual images as a strategic asset. Training programs should particularly focus on the way visual images can impact the sensitivities of indigenous populations. In his July 2010 *Small Wars Journal* article entitled "Throwing the Book at the Taliban: Undermining Taliban Legitimacy by Highlighting Their Own Hypocrisy," Colonel Greg Kleponis, U.S. Air Force Reserves, advocates the use of a proactive IO campaign based on indigenous culture as a keystone to successful counterinsurgency operations. A successful IO campaign begins with training. Such training should not only focus on the actions of the force providing opportunity for enemy propaganda, but also on use of visual images as potentially offensive or defensive weapons in the commander's campaign plan.

A 21st century commander should not be merely technically and tactically proficient. He or she must be media proficient and able to anticipate how audiences at home and abroad may interpret force actions. A PA officer may not be able to save an undisciplined commander who is not media savvy, or who ignores the power of images, or the necessity for training in this new environment. We must train a new type of service member (officer and enlisted) who is able to anticipate and understand the power that images can have in both the online and offline environment.

First, commanders must begin to think in terms of platforms, rather than computers. The digital age is as much a condition of the environment as the weather or geography. The Army must invest, even when resources are tight, in digital platforms and prepare to use them in a way that works to the benefit of the force and specific mission goals. Such investment is, and will continue to be, a force multiplier.

Second, commanders must consider that images reach multiple audiences in multiple ways. Presidents have long understood that, when they are speaking, they reach multiple audiences whether they intend to or not, and whether they want to or not. In the digital world, *everyone* is speaking to multiple audiences, a reality well worth incorporating into training as well. In presumed private forums, whatever was video-taped last night will end up on YouTube by morning. The old rule was "Don't email what you don't want to read on the front page of the paper." The new rule is "Don't videotape what you don't want on the world's smart phones." Where the U.S. military has been even weaker has been in communicating the rule's corol-lary: "*Do* photograph what you *do* want in public."

Finally, commanders must recognize that the meaning of an image is never intrinsic or permanent. Whether the enemy places an image in new contexts or an audience's perceptions of the image change over time, its meaning is fluid. We must therefore calibrate our response with that reality in mind. We must not confuse the shelf-life of the image with the shelf-life of the effect that image inspires. Rejecting short-term considerations for long-term viability must become a cornerstone of our thinking about a multi-mediated, visual environment.

REFERENCES

Andrew Tilghman, "Officials Troubled Over Behavior of Troops," *Army Times*, May 3, 2012. Available from *www.armytimes.com/article/20120503/NEWS/205030315/.*

Greg Kleponis, "Throwing the Book at the Taliban: Un-dermining Taliban Legitimacy by Highlighting Their Own Hypocrisy," *Small Wars Journal*, July 2010. Available from *smallwarsjournal.com/blog/journal/docs-temp/523-kleponis.pdf.*

ABOUT THE CONTRIBUTORS

MATT ARMSTRONG is an author, speaker, and strategist on issues related to international media and public diplomacy. He presently serves as a Member of the Broadcasting Board of Governors, a position he has held since confirmation by the Senate on August 1, 2013. In 2011, he served as executive director of the U.S. Advisory Commission on Public Diplomacy. Previously, Mr. Armstrong was an adjunct professor of public diplomacy at the Annenberg School of Journalism and Communication at the University of Southern California. In 2010, he founded and served as President of the MountainRunner Institute and published *www.mountainrunner.us*, a blog on public diplomacy and strategic communication. He is a member of the Board of Directors of the Public Diplomacy Council and a member of the International Institute of Strategic Studies. Mr. Armstrong holds a B.A. and an M.P.D. from the University of Southern California.

SAEID BELKASIM is an Associate Professor of Computer Science at Georgia State University. He is a well-known expert in pattern recognition and image processing, having published more than 60 articles in refereed journals and conference proceedings, whose research in pattern recognition and image processing has been cited in more than 700 articles. He has been a recipient of the prestigious International Pattern Recognition Society Honorable Mention award. Dr. Belkasim's research has earned him such recognition internationally that several of his published algorithms are now used as benchmarks for evaluating other methods: indeed, one of these popular benchmark algorithms is known as "Belkasim's method," an indication of the level of respect with which his work is treated among researchers in his field.

CORI E. DAUBER is a Professor of Communication Studies at the University of North Carolina at Chapel Hill, where she is also a Research Fellow at the Triangle Institute for Security Studies. From 2008 to 2012, she served as a Visiting Research Professor at the U.S. Army War College. Her research focuses on the media and information strategies of terrorist and insurgent groups. Dr. Dauber's most recent monograph is *YouTube War: Fighting in a World of Cameras in Every Cell Phone and Photoshop on Every Computer* (Strategic Studies Institute, U.S. Army War College, 2009). She has published in journals such as *Armed Forces and Society, Strategic Studies,* and *Rhetoric and Public Affairs,* and presented her work in a variety of forums, including the National Defense University, the John F. Kennedy School for Special Warfare, the NESA Strategic Institute, the U.S. Special Operations Command, and others.

JEFFRY R. HALVERSON is an Islamic studies scholar and historian of religions, specializing in the Middle East and North Africa. He currently serves as an assistant research professor in the Hugh Downs School of Human Communication at Arizona State University. Professor Halverson is the author of *Theology and Creed in Sunni Islam* (Palgrave Macmillan, 2010), *Searching for a King: Muslim Nonviolence and the Future of Islam* (Potomac, 2012), and the lead author of *Master Narratives of Islamist Extremism* (Palgrave Macmillan, 2011).

LOUIS H. JORDAN, JR., is a retired U.S. Army Colonel and former Deputy Director of the Strategic Studies Institute at the U.S. Army War College. He served in Afghanistan as Ministerial Advisor to the Deputy Minister of Interior for Counternarcotics. He is currently an Independent Consultant to the Chief of Staff of the Army Senior Fellows Program at the U.S. Army War College. Colonel Jordan's publications include *Cyber Infrastructure Protection VOL I and II* (Strategic Studies Institute, U.S. Army War College, 2009 and 2013), *Arms Control and European Security* (Strategic Studies Institute, U.S. Army War College, 2012), and *Counternarcotics Operations in Afghanistan; The COIN of the Realm*, (Point of Interest, Strategic Studies Institute Newsletter, 2010). He has appeared on *The Current with Anna Marie Tremonti*, Canadian Broadcasting Company, and given several presentations on the Afghan drug trade and counterinsurgency at Columbia University, George Washington University, and the Carnegie Council.

NATALIA MIELCZAREK is a third-year Ph.D. student at the University of Iowa. Her dissertation focuses on the production, selection, dissemination and impact of iconic news photographs in the digital and social media era. She is also interested in issues of censorship. Before she joined the Journalism and Mass Communication Department at the University of Iowa, Ms. Mielczarek worked for 10 years as a newspaper reporter.

DAVID D. PERLMUTTER is a Professor at and Dean of the College of Media and Communication at Texas Tech University, Lubbock, TX. He is the author or editor of nine books on political communication and persuasion including: *Photojournalism and Foreign Policy: Framing Icons of Outrage in International Crises* (Praeger, 1998); *Visions of War: Picturing Warfare from the Stone Age to the Cyberage* (St. Martin's Press, 1999); *From Pigeons to News Portals: Foreign Reporting and the Challenge of New Technology* (Louisiana State University Press, 2007); and *Blogwars: The New Political Battleground* (Oxford, UK, 2008). He has written several dozen research articles for academic journals such as *Orbis, Mass Communication* and the *Journal of Communication*, as well as more than 200 essays for U.S. and international newspapers and magazines. Mr. Perlmutter has been interviewed by most major news networks and newspapers, from *The New York Times* to CNN, ABC, and *The Daily Show*.

SHAWN POWERS is Assistant Professor at Georgia State University and an Associate Director at the Center on International Media Education. He previously served as a research fellow at the London School of Economics and Political Science, Oxford University's Program in Comparative Media and Law, and at the University of Pennsylvania's Annenberg Center for Global Communication Studies. Professor Powers' work has been published in journals including *Media, War and Conflict; Global Media and Communication; Ethnopolitics* and *Media Development*. He helped design and managed CPD's evaluation of Alhurra TV, and co-led projects for the World Bank and Deutsche Welle (on media development.) He co-directs the Annenberg-Oxford Summer Institute on Media, Law and Policy at Oxford University, UK, a summer program on Media and Globalization in Istanbul, Turkey, and is an occasional commentator for CNN International, *The Guardian*, and National Public Radio.

SCOTT W. RUSTON is currently an Assistant Research Professor with Arizona State University's Center for Strategic Communication, where he specializes in narrative theory and media studies. He combines these academic disciplines with his own past military experience to address real world problems of strategic communication. Professor Ruston is the co-author of *Narrative Landmines: Rumors, Islamist Extremism and the Struggle for Strategic Influence* (Rutgers University Press, 2012), and has presented widely on topics intersecting media, narrative/counter-narrative and terrorism.

ANNE STENERSEN is Research Fellow with the Terrorism and Political Violence Project at the Norwegian Defense Research Establishment (FFI). Trained in Middle Eastern studies, Arabic, and Russian, she has conducted research on militant Islamism, focusing on the al-Qaida network and its affiliates in Afghanistan and Pakistan. Ms. Stenersen's recent publications include: *Al Qaeda's Quest for Weapons of Mass Destruction: The History Behind the Hype* (Saarbrücken: VDM Verlag, February 2009); "The Internet: A Virtual Training Camp?" *Terrorism and Political Violence* (April 2008); "Chem-bio Cyber Class: Assessing Jihadist Chemical and Biological Manuals," *Jane's Intelligence Review* (September 2007); "Are the Afghan Taliban Involved in International Terrorism?" *CTC Sentinel,* (September 2009); and "The Taliban Insurgency in Afghanistan: Organization, Leadership and Worldview," *FFI Research Report* No. 2010/00359.

MICHAEL S. WALTMAN is an Associate Professor of Communication Studies at the University of North Carolina at Chapel Hill. His research is focused on the features and functions of hate discourse. Recently, Professor Waltman has published seven articles and book chapters on hate speech and co-authored (with John Haas) one book: *The Communication of Hate* (Peter Lang, 2011). This research has won several peer-reviewed awards including the Rose B. Johnson Award for Outstanding Article in *Southern Communication Journal* for 2003-04 and the Franklyn S. Haiman Award for Distinguished Scholarship in Freedom of Expression (A National Communication Association award).

CAROL K. WINKLER is Associate Dean of Humanities and Professor of Communication Studies at Georgia State University. She is the author of five books and more than 30 articles on the rhetoric of foreign policy and terrorism, visual communication, and argumentation. Dr. Winkler's most recent book, *In the Name of Terrorism: Presidents on Political Violence in the Post-World War II Era* (SUNY, 2006), won the National Communication Association's Outstanding Book Award in Political Communication. Her research on the relationship between visual images and ideology won that same organization's top research award for visual communication.

U.S. ARMY WAR COLLEGE

Major General William E. Rapp
Commandant

*****

STRATEGIC STUDIES INSTITUTE
and
U.S. ARMY WAR COLLEGE PRESS

Director
Professor Douglas C. Lovelace, Jr.

Director of Research
Dr. Steven K. Metz

Editors
Dr. Carol K. Winkler
Dr. Cori E. Dauber

Editor for Production
Dr. James G. Pierce

Publications Assistant
Ms. Rita A. Rummel

*****

Composition
Mrs. Jennifer E. Nevil

www.ingramcontent.com/pod-product-compliance
Lightning Source LLC
Chambersburg PA
CBHW080328270326

41927CB00014B/3131